PYTHON PROGRAMMING AND SQL

5 books in 1 - from Starter to Smarter. Master Hands-On Coding, Break Career Barriers, and Unlock Expert Techniques with a Step-by-Step Method

Alan P. Cochran

Dear Reader,

Thank you for choosing our book on Amazon. After countless hours and immense effort in its creation, your opinion is crucial to us. After the reading is complete, an honest review on Amazon would greatly benefit us as authors and other readers in their quest for quality books.

Your brief yet impactful review can make a big difference. We appreciate your support and are grateful for any feedback you may share.

Warm regards,

Alan P. Cochran

Table of Contents

BOOK 1: THE ESSENTIALS OF PYTHON PROGRAMMING..........................6

1.1 - INTRODUCTION:...7

WELCOME TO THE WORLD OF PYTHON AND SQL.............................7

An Overview of Python 7

SQL a Brief Introduction 12

1.2 - PYTHON BASICS: SETTING THE STAGE.................................17

Installing Python and Setting Up the Environment.........................17

Python Syntax 20

1.3 - ALGORITHMS AND LOGIC: PYTHON'S PERSPECTIVE............26

Unraveling Algorithms 26

Logical Thinking in Python 32

1.4 - HARDWARE AND SOFTWARE ESSENTIALS...........................40

Hardware 101 40

Software Foundations..47

BOOK 2: BUILDING BLOCKS AND PROGRAMMATIC STRUCTURE IN PYTHON . 52

2.1 - PYTHON'S TOOLKIT: SETUP AND FIRST PROGRAMS............53

Configuring Your Programming Environment..................................53

Hello World and Beyond 58

2.2 - PYTHON VARIABLES, DATA TYPES, AND STRUCTURES.........66

Grasping Variables 66

Data Types Unveiled..73

Lists, Tuples, and Dictionaries 77

2.3 - CONTROL FLOW AND DECISION MAKING IN PYTHON 85

Understanding If-Else Statements 85

For and While Statements 91

2.4 - DEEP DIVE INTO FUNCTIONS AND OBJECT-ORIENTED PYTHON PROGRAMMING 97

Function Fundamentals 97

Embracing Object-Oriented Principles in Python 106

Classes and Objects 113

BOOK 3: INTRODUCTION TO SQL AND DATABASE MANAGEMENT 122

3.1 - INTRODUCTION TO DATABASES AND SQL 123

Database Fundamentals 123

The Role of SQL 127

3.2 - FOUNDATIONAL SQL COMMANDS AND TECHNIQUES 129

SELECT, FROM, WHERE 129

Sorting and Filtering 133

INSERT, UPDATE, DELETE Operations 138

3.3 - SQL SERVERS AND INTERFACES 144

Exploring SQL Servers 144

User Interfaces for SQL 148

BOOK 4: ADVANCED SQL AND INTEGRATIVE TECHNIQUES 151

4.1 - ADVANCED SQL CONCEPTS AND PROCEDURES 152

Stored Procedures 152

DYNAMIC SQL.. 163

TRANSACTION MANAGEMENT 171

4.2 - INTEGRATIONS: ODBC, JDBC, XML, AND JSON IN SQL 182

OVERVIEW OF ODBC AND JDBC.. 182

SQL AND XML INTEGRATION 188

JSON IN SQL.. 194

BOOK 5: MASTERING INTEGRATION AND COMPLEX SOLUTIONS 200

5.1 - ADVANCED TECHNIQUES IN BOTH PYTHON AND SQL 201

PYTHON AND SQL INTEGRATION STRATEGIES... 201

LEVERAGING PYTHON LIBRARIES WITH SQL 208

REAL-WORLD APPLICATIONS OF INTEGRATED PYTHON AND SQL SOLUTIONS...... 214

5.2 - CONCLUSION: THE POWER OF PYTHON AND SQL: A JOURNEY'S END....... 223

REFLECTING ON THE LEARNING JOURNEY: MILESTONES AND ACHIEVEMENTS 223

THE FUTURE AWAITS: CONTINUING THE PYTHON AND SQL ADVENTURE 224

APPENDICES 226

PYTHON EXERCISES & PROJECTS 226

Hands-On Python Challenges: Applying Knowledge 226

Python Project Showcase: Building Practical Applications 229

SQL EXERCISES & PROJECTS... 232

SQL Skill Challenges: Testing Proficiency 232

Database Project Showcase: Integrating Skills into Real-world Scenarios........ 235

RECOMMENDED RESOURCES AND FURTHER READING 239

>> BONUS << 241

GLOSSARY OF TERMS 242

BOOK 1: THE ESSENTIALS OF PYTHON PROGRAMMING

1.1 - Introduction:

Welcome to the World of Python and SQL

Welcome to the fascinating intersection of Python and SQL, where the realms of programming and database management converge. This introduction sets the stage for your journey into the dynamic world of these two powerful technologies. As you embark on this learning adventure, you'll gain a holistic understanding of Python's versatile programming capabilities and SQL's prowess in handling databases.

An Overview of Python

Object-oriented programming is a high-level programming language that makes use of semantics. This language is at the high level. A high level is reached in terms of the structures that are present in the data, as well as the integration of dynamic typing and binding. The fact that it can be utilized for Rapid Application Development and for linking various aspects is what renders it an appealing option.

As a result of Python's ease of use and straightforward learning process, it is easier to comprehend the programming language. This is one of the reasons why Python serves to minimize the cost of maintaining the software. Python is a programming language that allows a variety of packages and modules, which enables it to promote modularity and code reuse inside programs. Binary representations of the standard library and the Python interpreter are both located on the internet. It is not required to charge charges for every one of the platforms that are accessible, and it could be supplied without cost.

Python is a popular programming language among programmers since it offers a high level of productivity. The cycle of edit-test-debug is a method that is both quick and doesn't involve any kind of compilation process. Python is a programming language that is easier to debug, and it does not result in any segmentation faults. An exception is thrown if the interpreter finds a mistake in the language being used. It is the interpreter's responsibility to print evidence whenever the program is not aware of the exception. On the level of sourcing, the debugger will make it possible to view any variables currently being used. There is going to be an adjustment of breakpoints, arbitrary expressions, and stepping on the code at any moment. This procedure will take place. It is Python that is responsible for writing the debugger, which is a simple and speedy way of debugging that involves placing prints on the source and statements.

Python, much like Perl and Ruby, is supported by several imaging programs, and users have the ability to write extensions that are tailored to their own needs. Blender and GIMP are two examples of web programs that support the Python application programming interface (API).

Both those who are just starting out in Python programming and those who have been doing it for a while will find this knowledge to be helpful. Most skilled developers can learn and utilize Python with relative ease. An easier method of installing Python is available, and most distributors of UNIX and Linux contain the most recent version of Python. Because of this, many PCs already have Python installed on them when they are purchased. You need to be aware of which integrated development environments (IDEs) and text editors are perfect for Python prior to you start utilizing it. You have the option of reading introductory books and code examples to acquire additional assistance and information. Following the development of the ABC language in 1980, the idea of Python was conceived. Python 2.0 included capabilities like as garbage collection and list comprehensions, both of which are utilized in reference cycle collection. These features were introduced when Python 2.0 was released. Python 3.0, which was published in 2008, was responsible for a comprehensive overhaul of the language. The most common applications for Python comprise the development of software and websites, as well as mathematical and scripting systems. While Python 2 continues to be widely used, Python 3 is the most recent version of the Python programming language. Python is a programming language that was intended to assist with reading and learning similar features of other languages, like English, with a particular focus on mathematics.

Unlike other programming languages, which often make use of semicolons, Python commands are finished with a new line. This contrasts with other languages. It is dependent on the definition of the scope, as well as indentation and whitespace.

Why Learn Python?

The neat thing about working with Python is that it has something for everyone to enjoy along the way. There are tons of benefits that come with it, and it really does not matter if you have worked with programming in the past or not. You will still find something to love about Python, and it is something that is easy to work with for all levels of programming. Some of the various reasons why you may want to work with the Python language overall comprise:

1. **It Has Some Code That Is Maintainable and Readable**

While you are writing out some of the applications for the software, you will need to focus on the quality of source code to simplify some of the updates and the maintenance. The syntax rules of Python are going to give you a way to express the concepts without having to write out any additional codes. At the same time, Python, unlike some of the other coding languages out there, is going to emphasize the idea of the readability of the code and can allow us to work with keywords in English instead of working with various types of punctuations to do that.

2. **Comes With Many Programming Paradigms**

Another benefit that we will see is the multiple programming paradigms. Like some of the other coding languages that we can find, Python is going to support more than one programming paradigm inside of it. This is going to be a language that can support structured and oriented programming to the fullest. In addition, a language will feature some support for various concepts when it comes to functional and aspect-oriented programming.

Along with all of this, the Python language is going to feature a kind of system that is dynamically typed and some automatic management of the memory. The programming paradigms and language features will help us to work with Python to develop complex and large software applications when we want to.

3. Compatible With Most Major Systems and Platforms

Right now, Python can support many various operating systems. It is even possible to work with interpreting to run the code on some of the specific tools and platforms that we want to use. In addition, since this is known as a language that is interpreted, it is going to allow us to go through and run the exact same code on many various platforms without the need of doing any recompilation.

Because of this, you are not required to recompile the code when you are done altering it. You can go through and run the application code that you modified without recompiling and check the impact of the changes that happened to that code right away. The feature makes it a lot easier to go through and make some changes to the code without having to worry about the development time along the way.

4. It Can Simplify Some of the Work That You Are Doing

Python is seen as a programming language that is general-purpose in nature. This means that you can use this language for all of the various processes and programs that you want to, from web applications to developing things like desktop applications as needed. We can even take it further and use this language to help develop complex scientific and numeric applications.

Python was designed with a lot of features that are there to facilitate the data analysis and visualizations that we will talk about in this guidebook. It is also possible to make use of these characteristics in Python in order to develop some individualized solutions for big data without requiring you to put in additional work or time.

As we can see, there are several benefits that we are able to enjoy when it comes to using the Python language, and this is just the beginning. As we go through and learn more about how to work in this language and what it can do for us, we will be able to see more and more of the benefits at the same time, and it will not take long working with your own data analysis to understand exactly how great this can be for our needs.

The Pythonic Philosophy

Python's design is guided by a set of principles commonly referred to as the "Pythonic" way. This philosophy emphasizes code readability, simplicity, and explicitness. The Zen of Python, a collection of aphorisms that capture the essence of Python's design principles, includes maxims like "Readability counts" and "Simple is better than complex."

The Pythonic philosophy extends beyond the code itself, influencing the community's ethos. Collaboration and openness are highly valued in the Python community, fostering an environment where developers are encouraged to share code, knowledge, and best practices.

Python in Action

Python's versatility is a key factor in its widespread adoption across various domains.

1. **Web Development**

Frameworks like Django and Flask have propelled Python to the forefront of web development. These frameworks provide robust tools for building scalable and secure web applications. Python's simplicity, combined with the power of these frameworks, makes it an ideal choice for both beginners and experienced developers in the web development realm.

2. **Data Science and Machine Learning**

Python's popularity in data science & machine learning is unrivaled. Libraries like NumPy, Pandas, and scikit-learn provide a powerful ecosystem for data manipulation, analysis, and machine learning. With the advent of deep learning frameworks like TensorFlow and PyTorch, Python has become the de facto language for AI and machine learning applications.

3. **Automation and Scripting**

Python's ease of use and readability make it a go-to choice for automation and scripting tasks. Whether it's automating repetitive tasks, managing files, or orchestrating system processes, Python excels in simplifying complex operations.

4. **Scientific Computing**

Scientists and researchers benefit from Python's capabilities in scientific computing.

Libraries like SciPy and Matplotlib offer tools for scientific computing, data visualization, and analysis, making Python a preferred language in academia and research.

SQL a Brief Introduction

SQL acts as the pivotal element in the field of database management, providing a standardized approach to interact with and manipulate relational databases.

Understanding SQL Fundamentals

1. **Data Definition Language (DDL)**

SQL is a domain-specific language that primarily consists of Data Definition Language (DDL) and Data Manipulation Language (DML).

DDL allows users to define and manage the structure of a database, comprising the creation, modification, and deletion of tables.

It sets the foundation for organizing and storing data in a structured manner.

```
CREATE TABLE Employees (
    EmployeeID INT PRIMARY KEY,
    FirstName VARCHAR(50),
```

```
   LastName VARCHAR(50),

   Age INT,

   Department VARCHAR(50)

);
```

In this instance, we use DDL to create a table named "Employees" with identified columns and their data types.

2. **Data Manipulation Language (DML)**

DML, on the other hand, focuses on interacting with the data stored in the database. It includes operations like querying, inserting, updating, and deleting data. Let's look at a simple SELECT statement to retrieve information from our "Employees" table:

```
SELECT FirstName, LastName, Age

FROM Employees

WHERE Department = 'IT';
```

This SQL query retrieves the first name, last name, and age of employees working in the IT department.

Unveiling the Power of SQL in Relational Databases

Relational databases organize data into tables, starting associations among them. SQL excels in managing these associations, enabling efficient data retrieval and manipulation.

1. **Joins for Relationship Navigation**

Joins enable the merging of rows from two or more tables by using a common or related column. For instance, to retrieve information about employees and their respective departments, you can use a JOIN operation:

```
SELECT Employees.FirstName, Employees.LastName, Departments.DepartmentName
```

```
FROM Employees

INNER JOIN Departments ON Employees.DepartmentID = Departments.DepartmentID;
```

This query combines information from the "Employees" and "Departments" tables depending on the common "DepartmentID" column.

2. Aggregating Data with GROUP BY

SQL offers powerful aggregation functions like COUNT, SUM, AVG, etc., combined with the GROUP BY clause. This allows you to summarize and analyze data at a higher level.

```
SELECT Department, AVG(Age) as AverageAge

FROM Employees

GROUP BY Department;
```

Here, we calculate the average age of employees in each department using the GROUP BY clause.

Integrating Python and SQL

The synergy between Python and SQL offers a potent combination for developers and data scientists. Python's versatility, coupled with SQL's database management capabilities, opens up a world of opportunities for building robust data-driven applications.

1. Python's Database Connectivity Libraries

Python offers various libraries, like SQLAlchemy and Psycopg2, facilitating seamless communication with SQL databases. These libraries enable you to execute SQL queries, fetch results, and integrate database operations into your Python scripts effortlessly.

```
import sqlalchemy as db


# Create a SQL engine
```

```python
engine = db.create_engine('sqlite:///example.db')


# Connect to the database

connection = engine.connect()


# Execute a SQL query

result = connection.execute('SELECT * FROM Employees')


# Fetch the results

for row in result:

    print(row)
```

2. Object-Relational Mapping (ORM)

ORM frameworks like SQLAlchemy allow you to interact with databases using Python classes, abstracting away the underlying SQL queries. This enhances code readability and maintainability.

```python
from sqlalchemy import create_engine, Column, Integer, String, ForeignKey

from sqlalchemy.orm import association, Session

from sqlalchemy.ext.declarative import declarative_base

Base = declarative_base()

class Employee(Base):

    __tablename__ = 'Employees'
```

```python
    EmployeeID = Column(Integer, primary_key=True)

    FirstName = Column(String(50))

    LastName = Column(String(50))

    Age = Column(Integer)

    Department = Column(String(50))


# Create an engine and bind the schema

engine = create_engine('sqlite:///example.db')

Base.metadata.create_all(engine)


# Create a session

session = Session(engine)

# Query the database using ORM

employees = session.query(Employee).filter_by(Department='IT').all()
```

1.2 - Python Basics: Setting the Stage

In this foundational chapter, we lay the groundwork for your Python journey.

From installation to navigating the language's syntax, you'll build a solid understanding of the essentials.

Installing Python and Setting Up the Environment

Embarking on your Python programming journey requires a solid foundation, starting with the installation of Python and the setup of a conducive development environment.

Step 1: Installing Python

Local Installation:

Windows:

1. Visit the official Python website and download the latest version of Python for Windows.

2. Run the installer and make sure to check the box that says "Add Python to PATH" during the installation process.

3. Click "Install Now" to complete the installation.

4. To verify the installation, open the command prompt and type python --version or python -V. You should see the installed Python version.

macOS:

1. macOS usually comes with Python pre-installed. However, it's recommended to use a package manager like Homebrew for a more up-to-date version.

2. Open Terminal and install Homebrew if you haven't already:

```
/bin/bash -c "$(curl -fsSL
https://raw.githubusercontent.com/Homebrew/install/HEAD/install.sh)"
```

3. Install Python using Homebrew:

```
brew install python
```

4. Verify the installation with python --version or python -V.

Linux (Ubuntu/Debian):

1. Open a terminal and update your package list:

```
sudo apt update
```

2. Install Python:

```
sudo apt install python3
```

3. Verify the installation with python3 --version or python3 -V.

Step 2: Setting Up a Virtual Environment

Using virtual environments is a best practice to isolate your project dependencies.

1. Install the virtualenv package:

```
pip install virtualenv
```

2. Establish a virtual environment within your project directory:

```
virtualenv venv
```

3. Activate the virtual environment:

- On Windows:
  ```
  .\venv\Scripts\activate
  ```
- On macOS/Linux:
  ```
  source venv/bin/activate
  ```

Your command prompt or terminal prompt should change to indicate the activated virtual environment.

Step 3: Exploring Cloud-Based Options

If you prefer a cloud-based development environment, platforms like Jupyter Notebooks, Google Colab, or Microsoft Azure Notebooks provide convenient options.

These platforms offer browser-based Python environments with pre-installed libraries and tools.

1. **Jupyter Notebooks:**

- Install Jupyter:

```
pip install jupyter
```

- Launch Jupyter Notebook:

```
jupyter notebook
```

This opens a Jupyter Notebook session in your web browser.

2. **Google Colab:**

- Visit Google Colab.
- Sign in with your Google account and create a new notebook.

Google Colab offers a ready-to-use Python environment with access to powerful resources.

3. Microsoft Azure Notebooks:

- Visit Microsoft Azure Notebooks.
- Sign in with your Microsoft account and create a new project.

Azure Notebooks offer a cloud-based Python environment with integration with other Microsoft services.

Python Syntax

The Elegance of Python Syntax

Python's syntax is renowned for its readability and simplicity, principles that form the core of the language's design philosophy. Guido van Rossum, the creator of Python, famously stated, "Code is read much more often than it is written." This ethos is reflected in Python's clean and expressive syntax, making it an ideal language for both beginners and experienced developers.

1. Indentation Rules

In Python, indentation is not just a stylistic choice; it is a fundamental aspect of the language's syntax. Python is a computer language that depends on indentation to determine the layout of the code, in contrast to many other programming languages that also utilize braces or keywords to separate code blocks. Consistent indentation is essential for the interpreter to understand the scope and hierarchy of statements.

Consider the following example, where indentation determines the block structure:

```
if True:

    print("This is indented")

    print("So is this")

print("This is not indented")
```

The indentation within the **if** block signifies the statements belonging to that block. The last **print** statement, not indented, falls outside the **if** block.

2. Variable Declarations

Dynamic Typing:

The programming language Python is dynamically typed, which means that it is not necessary to specify the data type of a variable outright. The data type is determined in a dynamic manner by the interpreter while the program is running. This flexibility simplifies code writing and allows for more agile development.

```python
my_variable = 10        # Integer

my_string = "Hello"     # String

my_float = 3.14         # Float

my_boolean = True       # Boolean
```

Variable Assignment:

In Python, variables are assigned values using the = operator. The variable name is on the left, and the value is on the right. You can reassign variables with various values, even of various types:

```python
x = 5
print(x)            # Output: 5
x = "Hello"
print(x)            # Output: Hello
```

3. **Comments**

Comments in Python are essential for providing additional information about the code. They begin with the # symbol and are ignored by the interpreter.

Comments contribute to code readability and help explain complex sections.

```python
# This is a single-line comment

"""

This is a
```

```
multi-line comment
"""
```

4. **Print Statement**

The **print()** function is a versatile tool for displaying output in Python. It can handle various data types, and you can format the output using various techniques.

```
print("Hello, World!")
```

5. **Data Types**

Basic Data Types:

Python supports several fundamental data types, comprising:

- **Integers (int):** Whole numbers without decimal points.

- **Floats (float):** Numbers with decimal points.

- **Strings (str):** Sequences of characters, enclosed in single or double quotes.

- **Booleans (bool):** Logical values representing True or False.

```
integer_variable = 42

float_variable = 3.14

string_variable = "Python"

boolean_variable = True
```

Complex Data Types:

Python also includes more complex data types, like:

- **Lists:** Ordered collections of items.

- **Tuples:** Immutable ordered collections.

- **Dictionaries:** Unordered collections of key-value pairs.

```
my_list = [1, 2, 3, 4, 5]

my_tuple = (1, "two", 3.0)

my_dict = {"name": "Alice", "age": 30, "city": "Wonderland"}
```

6. **String Manipulation**

Strings in Python are versatile and offer various methods for manipulation:

```
greeting = "Hello, World!"

# Length of the string
length = len(greeting)

# Concatenation
new_greeting = greeting + " Welcome to Python!"

# String formatting

formatted_greeting = f"Length: {length}, Greeting: {greeting}"
```

7. **Control Structures**

If-Else Statements:

Control structures like **if** and **else** are crucial for directing the flow of a program depending on conditions.

```
x = 10

if x > 5:
```

```
    print("x is greater than 5")
else:
    print("x is less than or equal to 5")
```

Loops:

Loops, like **for** and **while**, enable the repetition of code.

```
# For loop
for i in range(5):
    print(i)
# While loop
counter = 0
while counter < 5:
    print(counter)
    counter += 1
```

8. **Functions**

Functions allow you to encapsulate blocks of code for reuse. They are defined using the **def** keyword.

```
def greet(name):
    return f"Hello, {name}!"
result = greet("Alice")
print(result)   # Output: Hello, Alice!
```

9. Lists

There are a variety of data types that might be contained within lists, which are organized collections that are modifiable.

```python
my_list = [1, "two", 3.0, [4, 5]]

# Accessing elements

print(my_list[0])       # Output: 1

# Slicing

print(my_list[1:3])     # Output: ['two', 3.0]

# Modifying elements

my_list[0] = 10

print(my_list)          # Output: [10, 'two', 3.0, [4, 5]]
```

10. Dictionaries

Dictionaries are unordered collections that store data in key-value pairs.

```python
person = {

   "name": "Bob",        "age": 25,      "city": "Techland"

}

# Accessing values

print(person["name"])    # Output: Bob

# Modifying values

person["age"] = 26

print(person)            # Output: {'name': 'Bob', 'age': 26, 'city': 'Techland'}
```

1.3 - Algorithms and Logic: Python's Perspective

In this chapter, we delve into the core concepts of algorithms and logical thinking, viewing them through the lens of Python.

From the basics of algorithms to translating logical concepts into Python code, you'll develop a strong foundation in problem-solving and programming logic.

Unraveling Algorithms

Algorithms

Within the realm of computer science, an algorithm represents a precisely articulated, sequential process or a collection of guidelines crafted to address a particular issue or execute a specific computation. Think of it as a recipe—precise instructions that guide the computer in executing tasks with accuracy and efficiency.

Characteristics of Algorithms

1. **Input:** Algorithms take input, which is processed to produce the desired output.

2. **Definiteness:** Each step in an algorithm must be precisely defined and unambiguous.

3. **Finiteness:** An algorithm is required to conclude within a finite number of steps.

4. **Effectiveness:** Every operation in the algorithm must be basic and executable.

Algorithmic Design Principles

1. **Divide and Conquer:** This principle involves breaking down a problem into smaller, more manageable sub-problems. Solve these sub-problems individually, and combine their solutions to address the original problem. The classic example of this approach is the merge sort algorithm.

2. **Greedy Algorithms:** Greedy algorithms make locally optimal choices at each stage with the hope of finding a global optimum. While this approach does not guarantee the best solution in every case, it often produces satisfactory results. The classic example is Dijkstra's algorithm for finding the shortest path in a graph.

3. **Dynamic Programming:** In dynamic programming, a problem is solved by first reducing it down into a series of simpler sub problems that overlap with one another. Every one of these sub problems is solved just one time, and the solutions are saved for future reference. The famous example is the Fibonacci sequence calculation.

4. **Backtracking:** Backtracking is a trial-and-error approach where the algorithm attempts various choices and abandons paths that lead to incorrect solutions. Sudoku-solving algorithms often use backtracking.

5. **Randomized Algorithms:** These algorithms use a random element to introduce an element of chance into their decision-making process. Randomized algorithms are often employed in situations where an exact solution is computationally expensive or impractical.

Common Algorithms in Python

Now, let's delve into some common algorithms implemented in Python, showcasing their practical applications and importance in solving real-world problems.

1. **Sorting Algorithms**

Sorting is a fundamental operation in computer science. Python offers various sorting algorithms, each with its own strengths and use cases.

Bubble Sort:

Bubble Sort entails a straightforward sorting algorithm that iteratively navigates through a list, examines neighboring elements, and exchanges them if they are not in the correct order.

```python
def bubble_sort(arr):
```

```
    n = len(arr)

    for i in range(n):
        for j in range(0, n-i-1):
            if arr[j] > arr[j+1]:
                arr[j], arr[j+1] = arr[j+1], arr[j]
my_list = [64, 25, 12, 22, 11]
bubble_sort(my_list)
print("Sorted array:", my_list)
```

Merge Sort

Merge Sort employs a divide-and-conquer approach, wherein it partitions the input array into two halves, systematically sorts each half recursively, and subsequently combines the sorted segments.

```
def merge_sort(arr):
    if len(arr) > 1:
        mid = len(arr) // 2
        left_half = arr[:mid]
        right_half = arr[mid:]

        merge_sort(left_half)
        merge_sort(right_half)

        i = j = k = 0
```

```python
    while i < len(left_half) and j < len(right_half):
        if left_half[i] < right_half[j]:
            arr[k] = left_half[i]
            i += 1
        else:
            arr[k] = right_half[j]
            j += 1
        k += 1

    while i < len(left_half):
        arr[k] = left_half[i]
        i += 1
        k += 1

    while j < len(right_half):
        arr[k] = right_half[j]
        j += 1
        k += 1

my_list = [64, 25, 12, 22, 11]
merge_sort(my_list)
print("Sorted array:", my_list)
```

2. Searching Algorithms

Searching algorithms are employed to find a specific element within a collection of data.

Linear Search:

Linear Search sequentially checks each element in a list until a match is found or the entire list has been traversed.

```python
def linear_search(arr, target):
    for i in range(len(arr)):
        if arr[i] == target:
            return i
    return -1
my_list = [64, 25, 12, 22, 11]
target_element = 12
result = linear_search(my_list, target_element)
print(f"Element {target_element} found at index {result}" if result != -1 else f"Element {target_element} not found")
```

Binary Search

A search algorithm known as Binary Search is an effective method for locating a particular value within an organized collection. This method works by continually splitting the search area in half.

```python
def binary_search(arr, target):
    low, high = 0, len(arr) - 1

    while low <= high:
        mid = (low + high) // 2
        mid_element = arr[mid]

        if mid_element == target:
            return mid
        elif mid_element < target:
            low = mid + 1
        else:
            high = mid - 1

    return -1

my_list = [11, 12, 22, 25, 64]
target_element = 12
result = binary_search(my_list, target_element)
print(f"Element {target_element} found at index {result}" if result != -1 else f"Element {target_element} not found")
```

The Role of Algorithms in Problem Solving

In order to solve difficult problems in an effective manner, algorithms are an essential component. Whether it's sorting a list, searching for an item, or optimizing routes on a map, algorithms form the backbone of computational problem-solving.

Real-world Applications

1. **Sorting and Searching in Databases:** Database systems use sorting algorithms to organize and retrieve data efficiently. Searching algorithms enable quick data retrieval depending on specific criteria.

2. **Pathfinding in Maps:** Algorithms like Dijkstra's and A* are employed for finding the shortest path between two locations on a map, guiding navigation systems.

3. **Data Compression:** Algorithms like Huffman coding are utilized to compress data, reducing file sizes without compromising information.

4. **Machine Learning and AI:** Machine learning algorithms, like clustering and classification algorithms, are integral to the development of artificial intelligence systems.

5. **Network Routing:** Algorithms determine the most efficient routes for data transmission across networks, optimizing communication processes.

Logical Thinking in Python

Logical thinking is the backbone of effective problem-solving in programming. Being able to evaluate patterns, come up with structured solutions, and break down difficult problems into simpler elements are all necessary components of this talent. In the context of Python programming, logical thinking is manifested in algorithmic design, decision-making processes, and the translation of abstract concepts into code.

Key Aspects of Logical Thinking in Python

1. **Problem Decomposition:** In order to approach every aspect of an intricate issue separately, it is necessary to first break the issue down into smaller, simpler parts. This decomposition is the first step in crafting a logical solution.

2. **Pattern Recognition:** Identifying patterns within a problem or its potential solutions is a hallmark of logical thinking. Recognizing patterns enables you to leverage existing algorithms or create new ones tailored to the specific context.

3. **Algorithmic Design:** Logical thinking in Python involves designing algorithms, step-by-step procedures for solving a particular problem. Effective algorithms are both efficient and adaptable to a variety of scenarios.

4. **Decision-Making:** Logical thinking guides decision-making processes, helping you choose the most appropriate solution depending on the given conditions. This is crucial in implementing control structures like if-else statements.

5. **Abstraction:** Abstracting the essential details from a problem allows you to focus on the core logic without getting bogged down by unnecessary complexities. Abstraction is a key element in designing modular and reusable code.

Translating Concepts into Python Code

Let's explore the pragmatic dimensions of logical thinking within the context of Python.

We'll explore the step-by-step process of translating conceptualized problem-solving strategies into executable code.

Instance: Finding the Maximum Element in a List

Conceptualization:

Imagine you have a list of numbers, and you want to find the maximum element within that list.

The logical steps to achieve this are:

1. Set up a variable to hold the maximum value.

2. Iterate through each element in the list.

3. Evaluate each element against the existing maximum value.

4. Update the maximum value if a larger element is found.

5. After iterating through the entire list, the variable will hold the maximum value.

Python Code:

Let's translate these logical steps into Python code:

```python
def find_max_element(lst):

    # Step 1: Initialize a variable to store the maximum value.

    max_value = float('-inf')  # Start with negative infinity as the initial maximum value.

    # Step 2: Iterate through each element in the list.

    for element in lst:

        # Step 3: Compare each element with the current maximum value.

        if element > max_value:

            # Step 4: Update the maximum value if a larger element is found.

            max_value = element

    # Step 5: The variable now holds the maximum value.
```

```
    return max_value

# Instance Usage:

numbers = [12, 5, 27, 8, 19]

result = find_max_element(numbers)

print("The maximum element is:", result)
```

In this instance, the logical thinking process guided the creation of a Python function that efficiently finds the maximum element in a given list.

Exercise: Calculating the Fibonacci Sequence

Now, let's apply logical thinking to a classic problem: calculating the Fibonacci sequence.

Conceptualization:

The Fibonacci sequence is a numerical series in which each number is the sum of the two preceding ones, typically commencing with 0 and 1. The logical steps to calculate the Fibonacci sequence are:

1. Initialize variables to store the first and second numbers in the sequence.

2. Specify the number of terms in the sequence.

3. Use a loop to generate the subsequent numbers by summing the previous two.

4. Store the results in a list.

Python Code:

Now, let's translate these steps into Python code:

```
def fibonacci_sequence(n):

    # Step 1: Initialize variables to store the first and second numbers.
```

```python
    first, second = 0, 1

    # Step 2: Specify the number of terms in the sequence.

    fibonacci_list = [first, second]

    # Step 3: Generate subsequent numbers using a loop.

    for _ in range(2, n):

        next_term = first + second

        fibonacci_list.append(next_term)

        # Update variables for the next iteration.

        first, second = second, next_term

    # Step 4: Return the list containing the Fibonacci sequence.

    return fibonacci_list


# Instance Usage:

sequence_length = 8

result_sequence = fibonacci_sequence(sequence_length)

print(f"The Fibonacci sequence of length {sequence_length} is:", result_sequence)
```

In this exercise, logical thinking guided the creation of a Python function that generates the Fibonacci sequence.

Applying Logical Thinking to Real-World Problems

Logical thinking in Python extends beyond individual exercises and examples. It is a skill that empowers you to tackle real-world problems efficiently. Let's explore how logical thinking can be applied to solve more complex challenges.

Problem: Task Scheduler

Imagine you need to design a task scheduler that takes a list of tasks and their execution times as input. The goal is to efficiently schedule the tasks in a way that minimizes the total execution time. Here's how logical thinking can guide the solution:

Logical Steps:

1. Sort the tasks depending on their execution times in ascending order.

2. Schedule tasks in a way that prioritizes shorter execution times.

3. Calculate the total execution time.

Python Code:

Let's translate these steps into Python code:

```python
def task_scheduler(tasks):

    # Step 1: Sort tasks depending on execution times.

    sorted_tasks = sorted(tasks, key=lambda x: x[1])

    # Step 2: Schedule tasks to minimize total execution time.

    schedule = []

    total_execution_time = 0


    for task in sorted_tasks:

        schedule.append(task[0])

        total_execution_time += task[1]
```

```
# Step 3: Return the scheduled tasks and total execution time.

    return schedule, total_execution_time

# Instance Usage:

tasks_list = [("Task A", 5), ("Task B", 3), ("Task C", 8), ("Task D", 2)]

scheduled_tasks, total_time = task_scheduler(tasks_list)

print("Scheduled Tasks:", scheduled_tasks)

print("Total Execution Time:", total_time)
```

In this instance, logical thinking guided the creation of a Python function that efficiently schedules tasks to minimize total execution time.

Honing Your Logical Thinking Skills

As you continue to refine your logical thinking skills in Python, consider the following practical tips:

1. **Practice Regularly:** Regular practice is crucial for honing logical thinking skills. Address a diverse array of problems, spanning from straightforward exercises to more intricate challenges.

2. **Understand the Problem:** Before diving into code, ensure you have a clear understanding of the problem. Break down the problem into smaller components and recognize patterns or similarities with previously solved problems.

3. **Use Pseudocode:** Consider writing pseudocode prior to writing actual code. Pseudocode is an informal and high-level description outlining the operational principles of a computer program. It allows you to focus on the logic without getting bogged down by syntax.

4. **Collaborate and Discuss:** Engage in discussions with peers or mentors. Explaining your thought process and listening to others' approaches can provide valuable insights and broaden your perspective.

5. **Explore Different Solutions:** Don't settle for the first solution that comes to mind. Explore various approaches to the same problem. This not only enhances your problem-solving skills but also exposes you to diverse programming paradigms.

6. **Read Others' Code:** Reviewing code written by others, especially more experienced programmers, can offer new perspectives on logical thinking and coding styles.

1.4 - Hardware and Software Essentials

In this chapter, we explore the crucial interplay between hardware and software, providing you with a comprehensive understanding of the foundational components that support Python programming.

Hardware 101

Computers are intricate machines composed of various interconnected components, each playing a unique role in enabling the functionality we often take for granted. To comprehend how Python code gets executed, it's essential to familiarize ourselves with these key components:

1. **Central Processing Unit (CPU**

The CPU is the central processing unit, often referred to as the brain of the computer. It performs the actual computations and executes instructions stored in the computer's memory. Modern CPUs are highly sophisticated, with multiple cores and threads to handle parallel processing.

Key Aspects of the CPU:

- **Clock Speed:** The number of cycles that the central processing unit (CPU) is capable of executing in one sec is indicated by the clock speed, which is measured in gigahertz (GHz). In broad terms, there is a correlation between a greater clock speed and faster processing.
- **Cores and Threads:** CPUs can have multiple cores, each capable of handling its own set of tasks simultaneously. Threads allow for even more parallelism within each core.
- **Cache Memory:** The CPU has a small but extremely fast memory known as cache. It stores frequently accessed data and instructions to accelerate processing.

2. **Memory (RAM**

Random Access Memory (RAM) is volatile memory used by the computer to store active processes and data that are currently in use. Unlike permanent storage (like hard drives), RAM is much faster but loses its contents when the computer is powered off.

Characteristics of RAM:

- **Speed:** RAM is much faster than storage devices like hard drives or SSDs, providing quick access to data for the CPU.

- **Volatility:** Data in RAM is volatile, meaning it is erased when the power is turned off. This is in contrast to permanent storage, like hard drives, which retains data even when the computer is powered down.

3. **Storage**

Storage devices, like Hard Disk Drives (HDDs) & Solid State Drives (SSDs), provide persistent storage for data even when the computer is turned off. These devices store the operating system, applications, and long-term data.

Types of Storage Devices:

- **Hard Disk Drives (HDD):** HDDs are able to read and write data because they make use of magnetic storage and spinning disks. When it comes to big storage capacity, they are less expensive than solid-state drives (SSDs), however they are slower.

- **Solid State Drives (SSD):** Solid-state drives (SSDs) make use of flash memory, which enables them to provide higher read and write speeds in comparison to hard disk drives (HDDs). They are more expensive but offer improved performance, making them popular for system drives.

4. **Motherboard**

The motherboard serves as the primary circuit board, starting connections among all the components within a computer. It serves as the central nervous system, providing communication pathways for data transfer between the CPU, memory, storage, and other peripherals.

Components on the Motherboard:

- **CPU Socket:** The slot where the CPU is installed on the motherboard.
- **RAM Slots:** Connectors for installing RAM modules.
- **Peripheral Connectors:** Interfaces for connecting devices like USB ports, audio jacks, and networking ports.

5. **Power Supply Unit (PSU): Delivering Power**

The Power Supply Unit (PSU) converts electrical power from an outlet into a form that the computer's components can use. It offers power to the motherboard, CPU, GPU, and other peripherals.

Key Aspects of the PSU:

- **Wattage:** The power rating of the PSU, measured in watts. It determines how much power the PSU can deliver to the components.
- **Efficiency:** PSU efficiency indicates how well it converts input power to usable power. Higher efficiency results in less wasted energy.

6. **Graphics Processing Unit (GPU)**

The Graphics Processing Unit (GPU) is responsible for rendering images and videos.

While it is crucial for graphics-intensive tasks like gaming and video editing, some applications, comprising specific Python libraries, can leverage GPU parallelism for accelerated computation.

GPU Characteristics:

- **CUDA Cores:** In NVIDIA GPUs, CUDA cores are parallel processors that handle computation tasks. More CUDA cores often lead to better parallel processing performance.
- **VRAM (Video RAM):** Similar to system RAM, VRAM is dedicated memory on the GPU used for storing textures, frame buffers, and other graphics-related data.

How Hardware Impacts Python Programming

Understanding these hardware components is pivotal for Python programmers, as the performance of Python code can be influenced by the underlying hardware. Here's how:

1. **CPU Performance and Python Execution**

Python, as an interpreted language, relies heavily on the CPU for execution.

Tasks that involve complex computations, like mathematical calculations or data manipulation, benefit from a higher-performing CPU with multiple cores.

Libraries like NumPy, commonly used for numerical operations, can take advantage of multi-core CPUs to parallelize computations, significantly improving performance.

2. **Memory Usage and Efficiency**

Python programs use memory to store variables, data structures, and other runtime information. The amount of RAM available can impact the size and complexity of the data that can be processed.

Optimizing memory usage in Python is essential for efficient code execution.

Techniques like using generators instead of lists for large datasets or releasing unused memory with tools like the garbage collector contribute to better memory efficiency.

3. **Storage Speed and Program Loading**

The speed of storage devices affects the time it takes to load and save data. In scenarios where large datasets or files are involved, the choice between HDDs and SSDs can significantly impact the program's overall performance.

When working with Python programs that read or write large amounts of data, optimizing storage choices becomes crucial for efficient data handling.

4. **Parallelism with GPUs**

Certain Python libraries, like TensorFlow and PyTorch, are designed to leverage GPU parallelism for machine learning and deep learning tasks. Training large neural networks is computationally intensive, and GPUs with a high number of CUDA cores can significantly accelerate these operations.

When developing machine learning models in Python, understanding GPU capabilities and optimizing code for parallel processing becomes essential for achieving faster training times.

Best Practices for Python Performance Optimization

Now that we understand the impact of hardware on Python programming, let's explore some best practices for optimizing Python code for better performance:

1. **Use Efficient Data Structures**

Choosing the right data structures is crucial for efficient Python code. For example, using sets or dictionaries for membership tests can be much faster than lists, especially for large datasets.

```
# Inefficient
my_list = [1, 2, 3, 4, 5]
if 3 in my_list:
    print("Found")
```

```
# Efficient

my_set = {1, 2, 3, 4, 5}

if 3 in my_set:

  print("Found")
```

2. **Optimize Loops and Iterations**

Loops constitute a fundamental aspect of Python programming, and enhancing their efficiency can result in noteworthy performance improvements. Consider using built-in functions like **map()** and **filter()** instead of explicit loops for simple operations.

```
# Inefficient

result = []

for num in numbers:

  result.append(num * 2)

# Efficient

result = list(map(lambda x: x * 2, numbers))
```

3. **Use NumPy for Numerical Operations**

NumPy stands out as a potent library for numerical operations in Python, proficiently managing large arrays and matrices.

Leveraging NumPy can result in faster computations, especially for tasks involving mathematical operations on large datasets.

```
# Standard Python


result = [x + y for x, y in zip(list1, list2)]

# NumPy


import numpy as np

result = np.array(list1) + np.array(list2)
```

4. Take Advantage of Multi-Core CPUs

For tasks that can be parallelized, consider using libraries that support multi-core processing. The **concurrent.futures** module in Python offers a high-level interface for asynchronously executing callables, utilizing multiple cores.

```
from concurrent.futures import ThreadPoolExecutor

def process_data(data):

    # Some time-consuming operation

    return result

# Create a ThreadPoolExecutor with 4 workers

with ThreadPoolExecutor(max_workers=4) as executor:

    results = list(executor.map(process_data, my_data))
```

5. **Memory Management**

Efficient memory management is critical for Python performance. Avoid unnecessary data duplication and release memory promptly. Tools like **sys.getsizeof()** and memory profiling libraries can help identify memory-intensive areas in your code.

```
import sys

# Check the memory usage of a variable

memory_usage = sys.getsizeof(my_variable)
```

6. **Profile and Optimize**

Use profiling tools to identify bottlenecks in your code. The **cProfile** module in Python offers a built-in way to profile code and analyze its performance.

```
import cProfile

def my_function():

    # Your code here

# Profile the function

cProfile.run('my_function()')
```

Software Foundations

Version Control Systems (VCS)

Version Control Systems are essential tools for tracking changes in code, collaborating with others, and managing project history. They allow developers to work on various aspects of a project concurrently without conflicts. Here are two widely used version control systems:

1. **Git:** Git is a version control system that operates across multiple computers and allows for collaborative work. It enables numerous developers to work on a project at the same time and smoothly combine their modifications by combining their contributions. There are a number of platforms that offer hosting services for Git repositories, comprising GitHub, GitLab, and Bitbucket.

2. **Mercurial:** Mercurial is another distributed version control system similar to Git. It offers an easy-to-use interface and is known for its simplicity. While not as prevalent as Git, Mercurial is a suitable choice for projects where simplicity and ease of use are priorities.

Package Managers

Python package managers facilitate the installation, management, and distribution of Python packages. They ensure that your projects have the required dependencies and simplify the process of sharing code with others. The two main package managers for Python are:

1. **pip:** Pip serves as the primary package manager for Python, facilitating the installation, upgrading, and removal of Python packages. It accesses packages from the Python Package Index (PyPI), an extensive repository housing a wide array of Python packages.

```
# Instance: Installing a package

pip install package_name
```

2. **Conda:** Conda is an open-source package management and environment management system. It can install packages from the Anaconda repository or other channels. Conda is often used in conjunction with the Anaconda distribution, which includes a curated set of data science packages.

```
# Instance: Creating a Conda environment

conda create --name myenv python=3.8
```

Virtual Environments

Virtual environments enable the creation of isolated spaces for Python projects, each equipped with its unique set of dependencies. This ensures that various projects can have various package versions without conflicts. Two popular tools for managing virtual environments are:

1. **venv:** Venv is a built-in module in Python 3.3 and later versions that offers support for creating lightweight, isolated Python environments. It is simple to use and serves the basic needs of most projects.

```
# Instance: Creating a virtual environment with venv

python -m venv myenv
```

2. **virtualenv:** Virtualenv is a third-party tool that offers more features than venv. It supports both Python 2 and 3, providing extra configuration options for environments.

```
# Instance: Creating a virtual environment with virtualenv

virtualenv myenv
```

Continuous Integration (CI) and Continuous Deployment (CD)

Continuous Integration and Continuous Deployment are practices that involve automatically testing and deploying code changes. CI/CD tools help ensure code quality, reduce bugs, and streamline the deployment process. Two popular CI/CD platforms are:

1. **Jenkins:** An open-source automation server, Jenkins facilitates the building, deployment, and automation of diverse projects. It seamlessly integrates with various version control systems and offers plugins tailored for Python projects.

2. **Travis CI:** Travis CI is a cloud-based CI service that integrates with GitHub repositories. It automatically builds and tests code changes, providing feedback to

developers. Travis CI supports Python projects and is widely used in the open-source community.

Documentation Tools

Effective software development relies heavily on comprehensive documentation. Proper documentation makes code more accessible to others and ensures that future maintainers can understand the project. Here are two popular documentation tools for Python:

1. **Sphinx:** Sphinx is a documentation generator that simplifies the creation of intelligent and beautiful documentation. It supports multiple output formats, comprising HTML, PDF, and ePub. Sphinx is widely used for documenting Python projects.

```
# Instance: Generating documentation with Sphinx

sphinx-quickstart
```

2. **MkDocs:** MkDocs is a fast and simple documentation generator that focuses on creating project documentation in a clean and concise format. It uses Markdown files for documentation and is easy to set up.

```
# Instance: Creating documentation with MkDocs

mkdocs new my-project
```

Collaboration Platforms

Collaboration platforms provide a centralized space for team communication, project management, and code collaboration. They enhance coordination among team members and help streamline workflows. Two widely used collaboration platforms are:

1. **GitHub:** GitHub is a web-centric platform providing version control, project management, and collaboration functionalities. It hosts Git repositories, making it a popular choice for open-source projects and private repositories.

2. **GitLab:** GitLab is an online platform designed for managing Git repositories, offering source code management, continuous integration, and collaboration functionalities. Users can opt for either the cloud-based service or the self-hosted alternative.

BOOK 2: BUILDING BLOCKS AND PROGRAMMATIC STRUCTURE IN PYTHON

2.1 - Python's Toolkit: Setup and First Programs

In this chapter, we focus on setting up your Python development environment and taking your first steps in writing Python programs.

Configuring Your Programming Environment

Choosing the Right Text Editor

A text editor is the most basic tool for writing and editing code. While not as feature-rich as integrated development environments (IDEs), text editors offer simplicity, speed, and flexibility. Here are some popular text editors for Python development:

1. **Visual Studio Code (VSCode):** VSCode is a lightweight, open-source code editor developed by Microsoft. It offers impressive support for Python development through extensions. VSCode features syntax highlighting, linting, debugging, and an integrated terminal. Its extensive extension ecosystem allows you to tailor the editor to your specific needs.

2. **Atom:** Atom is a customizable, open-source text editor developed by GitHub. It supports Python development through packages and extensions. Atom's user-friendly interface and ease of customization make it a popular choice among developers.

3. **Sublime Text:** Sublime Text is a versatile text editor known for its speed and responsiveness. While it lacks built-in Python-specific features, its vast plugin ecosystem allows you to enhance its functionality for Python development. Sublime Text is available for free, but a license is required for continued use.

4. **Notepad++:** Notepad++ is a free, open-source text editor for Windows. It offers a range of features, comprising syntax highlighting for various programming languages,

comprising Python. Notepad++ is lightweight and fast, making it suitable for quick edits and small projects.

Integrated Development Environments (IDEs)

Integrated Development Environments (IDEs) provide a comprehensive suite of tools for software development. They typically comprise code editors, debugging tools, and features for project management. Here are some popular IDEs for Python development:

1. **PyCharm:** Developed by JetBrains, PyCharm is a powerful IDE specifically designed for Python development. It comes in two editions: Community (free) & Professional (paid). PyCharm offers features like intelligent code completion, project navigation, integrated testing, and debugging tools. It is widely used for both small scripts and large-scale projects.

2. **Spyder:** Spyder is an integrated development environment (IDE) that is open-source and built for scientific computing and data processing. NumPy, SciPy, and Matplotlib are just few of the well-known libraries that it interacts with without any problems. Spyder offers features like an interactive console, variable explorer, and support for IPython.

3. **Jupyter Notebooks:** Jupyter Notebooks provide an interactive computing environment suitable for data analysis, visualization, and machine learning. While not a traditional IDE, you are able to generate and share documents which include live code, equations, visualizations, and narrative text through the use of Jupyter Notebooks. The fields of data science and research all make extensive use of Jupyter.

4. **Visual Studio (VS):** Visual Studio is a comprehensive IDE developed by Microsoft. While it supports various programming languages, comprising Python, it is particularly powerful for .NET development. Visual Studio offers a rich set of features, comprising a powerful code editor, debugging tools, and support for web development.

Setting Up Your Python Environment

Configuring your Python environment involves installing the Python interpreter, managing dependencies, and creating virtual environments. Here are the key steps to set up your Python environment:

1. **Install Python**

Begin by installing the Python interpreter on your machine. You can download the latest version of Python from the official Python website. The website offers installers for various operating systems.

2. **Install a Package Manager**

Python comes with a built-in package manager called **pip**. However, for more advanced package management and environment control, you might consider using **conda**. Conda is a package manager and environment management system that simplifies the installation of dependencies.

```
# Instance: Installing a package with pip

pip install package_name

# Instance: Creating a Conda environment

conda create --name myenv python=3.8
```

3. **Set Up Virtual Environments**

Virtual environments are isolated environments that allow you to manage project-specific dependencies. They prevent conflicts between various projects by providing each project with its own set of libraries. The built-in **venv** module is available in Python 3.3 and later versions.

```
# Instance: Creating a virtual environment with venv

python -m venv myenv
```

4. **Activate the Virtual Environment**

Once the virtual environment is created, you need to activate it prior to working on your project. Activation sets the virtual environment as the current environment for your terminal or command prompt.

```
# Instance: Activating a virtual environment

# On Windows

myenv\Scripts\activate


# On macOS/Linux

source myenv/bin/activate
```

5. **Install Project Dependencies**

With the virtual environment activated, you can use **pip** to install project-specific dependencies. This ensures that your project has the required packages without affecting the global Python environment.

```
# Instance: Installing project dependencies

pip install -r requirements.txt
```

Configuring Your IDE for Python Development

Once you have chosen an IDE or text editor and set up your Python environment, it's time to configure your development environment for optimal Python coding. Here are some configuration tips for popular IDEs:

PyCharm

PyCharm is known for its powerful features tailored for Python development. Here are some configuration tips:

Configure Python Interpreter:

- Navigate to "Settings" or "Preferences."
- Under "Project: [Your Project Name]," select "Python Interpreter."
- Choose the Python interpreter associated with your virtual environment.

Code Style and Formatting:

- Customize code style and formatting preferences by navigating to "Settings" or "Preferences" > "Code Style" > "Python."

Configure Version Control:

- If you're using version control, configure it by navigating to "Settings" or "Preferences" > "Version Control."

Visual Studio Code (VSCode)

VSCode is a lightweight and extensible code editor. Here are some configuration tips for Python development:

Configure Python Interpreter:

- Install the "Python" extension from the VSCode marketplace.
- Use the "Select Python Interpreter" command to choose the interpreter associated with your virtual environment.

Extensions and Themes:

- Explore the VSCode marketplace for Python-related extensions and themes that suit your preferences.

Configure Settings:

- Customize settings by navigating to "Settings" > "Preferences."

Spyder

Spyder is tailored for scientific computing and data analysis. Here are some configuration tips:

Configure Python Interpreter:

- Set the Python interpreter in Spyder by navigating to "Tools" > "Preferences" > "Python Interpreter."

Adjust Preferences:

- Customize preferences in "Tools" > "Preferences" to match your coding style and preferences.

Jupyter Notebooks

Jupyter Notebooks provide an interactive computing environment. Here are some configuration tips:

Install Jupyter Extensions:

- Enhance Jupyter Notebooks by installing extensions through the Jupyter Contributed Extensions.

Configure Themes:

- Customize the appearance of Jupyter Notebooks by exploring available themes.

Hello World and Beyond

The journey into the world of Python programming begins with a single, iconic phrase: "Hello, World!" This simple program, often the first line of code written in any programming language, serves as a rite of passage for aspiring developers. However, our exploration doesn't stop there.

The Hello World Program

Let's commence with the quintessential "Hello, World" program. In Python, achieving this introductory milestone is remarkably straightforward. Open your text editor or integrated development environment (IDE) of choice and type the following:

```
# hello_world.py

print("Hello, World!")
```

Here's what each line does:

- **# hello_world.py**: This is a comment. The Python interpreter doesn't execute comments, yet they offer valuable information for developers. In this case, it indicates the name of the Python file.

- **print("Hello, World!")**: This line uses the **print()** function to display the text "Hello, World!" in the console. The **print()** function is a fundamental tool for outputting information in Python.

Save the file with a **.py** extension, like **hello_world.py**. To run it, open a terminal or command prompt, navigate to the file's directory, and execute:

```
python hello_world.py
```

Congratulations! You've just executed your first Python program. The "Hello, World" tradition serves as a foundational step, verifying that your Python environment is configured correctly and ready for more advanced coding endeavors.

Understanding Python Syntax

Python syntax is designed to be readable and expressive, making it an ideal language for beginners. Let's explore some fundamental building blocks of Python syntax:

1. **Indentation**

Unlike many programming languages that use braces **{}** or keywords to indicate code blocks, Python uses indentation. Proper indentation is not just a matter of style; it is a crucial aspect of Python syntax and affects how the code is executed.

```python
# Proper indentation
if True:
    print("This is indented")


# Improper indentation (will result in an error)
if True:
print("This is not indented")
```

2. **Variables and Data Types**

Variables are containers that are used to store the values of data. When working with Python, it is not necessary to set the type of the variable directly; Python infers it depending on the assigned value. Here are some common data types:

```python
# Integer
age = 25

# Float (floating-point number)
height = 1.75

# String
name = "Alice"

# Boolean
is_student = True
```

3. Comments

Comments provide additional information within the code. In Python, comments start with the # symbol and continue to the end of the line.

```
# This is a single-line comment


"""

This is a

multi-line comment

"""
```

4. Conditional Statements

Conditional statements allow the execution of various code blocks depending on identified conditions.

```
# Instance of an if statement

x = 10

if x > 5:

    print("x is greater than 5")
```

5. Loops

Loops are used to repeatedly execute a block of code. Python supports **for** and **while** loops.

```
# Instance of a for loop

for i in range(5):

    print(i)
```

6. Functions

Functions are blocks of reusable code. You can define your functions or use built-in ones.

```python
# Instance of a function

def greet(name):

    print(f"Hello, {name}!")

# Call the function

greet("Bob")
```

Variables and Dynamic Typing in Python

Because Python uses dynamic typing, it is not necessary to specify the type of a variable using the explicit declaration method. The interpreter determines the type dynamically depending on the assigned value. This flexibility can be advantageous but requires vigilance to avoid unexpected behaviors.

```python
# Dynamic typing example

x = 10      # x is an integer

x = "hello"  # x is now a string
```

While dynamic typing offers flexibility, it's crucial to be mindful of variable types, especially in larger programs where code maintenance becomes more complex.

Input and Output in Python

Interacting with users through input and output is fundamental. Python offers the **input()** function for user input and the **print()** function for output.

```python
# Input example

name = input("Enter your name: ")
```

```
print(f"Hello, {name}!")
```

This simple program prompts the user to enter their name and then greets them. The **input()** function returns the user's input as a string.

Building on the Basics

Now that you've grasped the fundamentals, let's build on them by creating a few practical programs. These examples will not only reinforce your understanding but also demonstrate the versatility of Python.

1. **Calculator Program**

```python
# Simple calculator program

def calculator():

    num1 = float(input("Enter the first number: "))

    operator = input("Enter the operator (+, -, *, /): ")

    num2 = float(input("Enter the second number: "))

    if operator == "+":

        result = num1 + num2

    elif operator == "-":

        result = num1 - num2

    elif operator == "*":

        result = num1 * num2

    elif operator == "/":

        if num2 != 0:

            result = num1 / num2
```

```python
    else:
        result = "Error: Division by zero"
    else:
        result = "Error: Invalid operator"


    print(f"Result: {result}")


# Call the calculator function
calculator()
```

This calculator program takes user input for two numbers and an operator, then performs the corresponding operation.

2. **Guess the Number Game**

```python
# Guess the number game
import random


def guess_the_number():
    secret_number = random.randint(1, 100)
    attempts = 0


    while True:
        guess = int(input("Enter your guess (1-100): "))
```

```python
        attempts += 1

        if guess == secret_number:

            print(f"Congratulations! You guessed the number in {attempts} attempts.")

            break
        elif guess < secret_number:

            print("Too low! Try again.")
        else:

            print("Too high! Try again.")


# Play the game

guess_the_number()
```

This game generates a random number between 1 & 100 and challenges the player to guess it. The program offers feedback on each guess until the correct number is guessed.

2.2 - Python Variables, Data Types, and Structures

In this chapter, we delve into the fundamental building blocks of Python programming—variables, data types, and structures.

Grasping Variables

In programming, a variable is a symbolic name that represents a location in memory where a value is stored. This value can be a number, a string of text, a boolean (True or False), or more complex data structures. Variables act as placeholders, allowing you to work with and manipulate data within your programs. Python variables are dynamically typed, which means that you do not need to specifically state their kind in order to modify them. On the basis of the value that has been given, the interpreter will decide the type. This flexibility makes Python versatile but requires vigilance to ensure that variables hold the expected types.

Naming Variables

Selecting relevant and descriptive names for your variables is essential when aiming to create code that is both clear and easy to maintain. Follow these best practices and conventions when naming variables in Python:

1. **Descriptive and Readable**

Choose names that convey the purpose of the variable. A name like **total** is more descriptive than **t**, making your code more readable and understandable.

```
# Good variable name

total_amount = 1000

# Less descriptive variable name

t = 1000
```

2. Use Camel Case for Multi-Word Names

When a variable name consists of multiple words, use camel case. This involves capitalizing the first letter of each word, excluding the initial one.

```
# Camel case

averageScore = 85
```

3. Avoid Single-Letter Names

While single-letter variable names (e.g., **x, y, z**) are common in mathematical contexts, it's advisable to use more meaningful names in other situations. Exceptions are often made for short-lived loop counters.

```
# Better than using single-letter names

for i in range(5):
  print(i)
```

4. Be Mindful of Keywords

Avoid using Python keywords as variable names. Keywords are reserved words with specific meanings in the language.

```
# Invalid variable name

class = "Python"

# Error: "class" is a keyword
```

5. Follow PEP 8

PEP 8 is the Python Enhancement Proposal that offers style guide recommendations for writing clean and readable code. Following PEP 8 ensures consistency across Python projects.

6. Use Underscores for Constants

If you have constants in your code, use uppercase letters and underscores to separate words.

```
# Constant variable

MAX_VALUE = 100
```

Following these naming conventions enhances code readability and maintainability, simplifying comprehension and collaboration for both yourself and others engaged in project work.

Assigning Values to Variables

Assigning values to variables is a straightforward process in Python. The assignment operator (=) is used for this purpose. The syntax is as follows:

```
variable_name = value
```

Here's an example:

```
# Assigning values to variables

name = "Alice"

age = 25

is_student = True
```

In this instance, three variables (**name**, **age**, and **is_student**) are assigned values—a string, an integer, and a boolean, respectively. Python automatically determines the type of each variable depending on the assigned value.

Multiple Assignments

Python lets you to assign values to multiple variables in a single line.

```
# Multiple assignments
```

```
x, y, z = 5, 10, 15
```

This line of code assigns the values 5, 10, and 15 to variables **x**, **y**, and **z**, respectively. This feature offers a concise way to initialize multiple variables.

Simultaneous Assignment

Python also supports simultaneous assignment, allowing you to swap values between variables without the need for a temporary variable.

```
# Simultaneous assignment

a, b = 10, 20

a, b = b, a

print(a, b)  # Output: 20 10
```

In this instance, the values of **a** and **b** are swapped in a single line.

Variable Scope and Lifetime

Understanding the scope & lifetime of variables is crucial for writing bug-free and maintainable code. In Python, the scope of a variable determines where it can be accessed or modified. The length of time that a variable remains stored in memory is referred to as its length of existence.

Global Scope

Variables declared without any specific function or block scope possess a global scope, enabling accessibility from any part of the code.

```
# Global variable

global_var = 100

def print_global():
```

```
    print(global_var)

print_global()  # Output: 100
```

Local Scope

The variables that have been assigned inside a function have a local scope, which means that they can only be accessed without leaving the function.

```
# Local variable
def print_local():
    local_var = 50
    print(local_var)
print_local()  # Output: 50
# Attempting to access local_var outside the function will result in an error
```

Lifetime of Variables

The lifetime of a variable is determined by when it is created and when it is destroyed. Global variables typically have a longer lifetime than local variables.

Instance of Variable Lifetime:

```
# Variable lifetime example
def variable_lifetime():
    x = 10  # x is created when the function is called
    print(x)
    # The function ends, and x is destroyed
variable_lifetime()
# Attempting to access x here will result in an error
```

Understanding variable scope and lifetime helps you avoid unexpected behavior, like unintentional modification of global variables within functions.

Best Practices for Using Variables

To ensure code clarity and maintainability, consider the following best practices when working with variables in Python:

1. Use Descriptive Names

Choose names that clearly convey the purpose of the variable. This makes your code self-documenting.

```python
# Descriptive variable names

total_amount = 1000
```

2. Avoid Magic Numbers

Avoid using "magic numbers" (hard-coded numerical values) in your code. Instead, assign them to named variables.

```python
# Magic number

total_cost = 500 * 1.15

# Improved version

tax_rate = 0.15

total_cost = 500 * (1 + tax_rate)
```

3. Refactor Code for Reusability

Identify common patterns in your code and refactor them into functions or classes to promote reusability.

```python
# Without refactoring

total_1 = 10 * 2

total_2 = 15 * 2
```

```python
# With refactoring

def calculate_total(quantity):

    return quantity * 2

total_1 = calculate_total(10)

total_2 = calculate_total(15)
```

4. **Keep Variable Scope in Mind**

Be conscious of variable scope to avoid unintended side effects or conflicts.

```python
# Global variable

total_amount = 1000

def update_total():

    # Avoid modifying global variables within functions if possible

    global total_amount

    total_amount += 50

update_total()

print(total_amount)  # Output: 1050
```

5. **Document Your Code**

Include comments or docstrings to explain the purpose of variables, especially in complex or collaborative projects.

```python
# Good use of comments

# Calculate the total cost comprising tax

total_cost = base_cost * (1 + tax_rate)
```

Data Types Unveiled

Numeric Types

1. Integers (int)

Integers signify whole numbers without any decimal points. In Python, integers can be positive, negative, or zero.

```
# Integers

positive_integer = 42

negative_integer = -10

zero = 0
```

Python's integers have unlimited precision, allowing you to work with very large numbers without worrying about overflow.

2. Floating-Point Numbers (float)

Floating-point numbers, or floats, signify numbers with decimal points. They allow the representation of a broader range of values, comprising fractional numbers.

```
# Floating-point numbers

pi = 3.14

gravity = 9.8
```

It's essential to note that floats have limited precision due to the way computers signify real numbers. This can sometimes lead to rounding errors.

3. Complex Numbers (complex)

Complex numbers have both a real and an imaginary part, denoted by the suffix **j**.

```
# Complex numbers
```

```
complex_number = 2 + 3j

another_complex = -1.5 - 2.5j
```

Complex numbers find applications in various mathematical and engineering domains, particularly in signal processing and electrical engineering.

Strings (str)

In Python, strings consist of character sequences and play a crucial role in managing textual data.

1. Creating Strings

You can form strings in Python using either single (') or double (") quotes.

```
# Single-quoted string

single_quoted = 'Hello, Python!'

# Double-quoted string

double_quoted = "Python is versatile."
```

Using single or double quotes allows flexibility when dealing with strings that contain one type of quote or the other.

2. Multiline Strings

Triple quotes ("'" or """) are used to create multiline strings.

```
# Multiline string

multiline_string = '''This is a

multiline string.'''
```

Multiline strings are handy for documenting code or representing longer textual content.

3. **String Concatenation**

Strings can be concatenated using the + operator.

```
# String concatenation

first_name = "John"

last_name = "Doe"

full_name = first_name + " " + last_name
```

String concatenation is a common operation when building dynamic strings.

4. **String Methods**

Strings in Python come with a plethora of built-in methods for various operations, like converting case, splitting, and joining.

```
# String methods

sentence = "Python is an amazing language."

uppercase_sentence = sentence.upper()

words = sentence.split()

joined_sentence = " ".join(words)
```

Understanding string methods enhances your ability to manipulate and process textual data efficiently.

Boolean Type

Boolean values signify truth or falsehood and are a crucial aspect of control flow in Python.

```
# Boolean

is_python_fun = True
```

```
is_learning = False
```

Booleans are essential for making decisions in your code using conditional statements.

1. **None Type: The Absence of a Value (None)**

The **None** type represents the absence of a value or a null value in Python.

```
# None type

no_value = None
```

It is often used to signify that a variable or function returns nothing or has no assigned value.

2. **Categorical Type: Enumerations (enum)**

Enumerations provide a way to create named constant values that signify members of a set.

```
# Enumeration

from enum import Enum

class Color(Enum):

    RED = 1

    GREEN = 2

    BLUE = 3
```

Enumerations enhance code readability by providing meaningful names to specific values.

Data Type Conversion

In Python, data type conversion allows you to transform one type into another. This can be essential when performing operations that require matching types or when receiving data of uncertain types.

1. **Implicit Type Conversion**

Python is capable of doing indirect type conversion, which is also referred to as coercion, in specific circumstances.

```
# Implicit type conversion
result = 10 + 3.5
```

In this instance, the integer **10** is implicitly converted to a float to perform the addition.

2. **Explicit Type Conversion**

You can explicitly convert between data types using built-in functions like **int()**, **float()**, **str()**, etc.

```
# Explicit type conversion
age = int("25")
pi = float("3.14")
```

Explicit type conversion is crucial when dealing with user inputs or data from external sources.

Lists, Tuples, and Dictionaries

Lists

Lists in Python are dynamic arrays, providing a versatile and mutable way to store ordered collections of items. They are possibly one of the data structures that are utilized the most frequently and are the most adaptable.

1. **Creating Lists**

Square brackets are employed to define lists, and commas are used to separate elements within the list.

```
# Creating a list

fruits = ['apple', 'banana', 'orange']
```

Lists exhibit high adaptability as they can accommodate elements of various data types.

2. Accessing Elements

Accessing elements in a list is done using indexing. Python uses zero-based indexing, meaning the first element is at index **0**.

```
# Accessing elements

first_fruit = fruits[0]

second_fruit = fruits[1]
```

Negative indexing is also supported, allowing you to access elements from the end of the list.

```
# Negative indexing

last_fruit = fruits[-1]

second_last_fruit = fruits[-2]
```

3. Modifying Lists

Lists are mutable, meaning you can modify their elements.

```
# Modifying elements

fruits[0] = 'pear'
```

You can also manipulate lists using various methods like **append()**, **insert()**, **remove()**, and more.

```
# Modifying lists with methods

fruits.append('grape')
```

```
fruits.insert(1, 'kiwi')
```

```
fruits.remove('banana')
```

4. List Slicing

List slicing allows you to create sublists by specifying a range of indices.

```
# List slicing
selected_fruits = fruits[1:3]
```

This operation creates a new list containing elements from index **1** (inclusive) to index **3** (exclusive).

5. Common List Operations

Lists support a variety of operations, comprising checking membership, finding the length, and concatenating.

```
# Common list operations
is_banana_in_list = 'banana' in fruits
list_length = len(fruits)
combined_list = fruits + ['mango', 'pineapple']
```

6. List Comprehensions

It is possible to generate lists in a single line using list comprehensions, which are a compact method.

```
# List comprehension
squared_numbers = [x**2 for x in range(5)]
```

This example creates a list of squared numbers from **0** to **4** using a list comprehension.

Lists are suitable for scenarios where you need a collection of items with a specific order and require flexibility in terms of adding, removing, or modifying elements.

Tuples

Unlike lists, tuples are immutable, which means that their components cannot be altered once they have been created. This is a significant difference between the two types of data structures.

Tuples are ideal for situations where data should remain constant.

1. **Creating Tuples**

Tuples are defined using parentheses, and elements within the tuple are separated by commas.

```
# Creating a tuple

coordinates = (10, 20)
```

2. **Accessing Elements**

Accessing elements in a tuple is done using indexing, similar to lists.

```
# Accessing elements

x_coordinate = coordinates[0]

y_coordinate = coordinates[1]
```

3. **Immutability**

Once a tuple is created, its elements cannot be changed.

```
# Attempting to modify a tuple (will result in an error)

coordinates[0] = 15
```

This immutability ensures that the data signified by the tuple remains constant throughout the program.

4. Unpacking Tuples

Tuples support unpacking, allowing you to assign multiple variables in a single line.

```
# Unpacking a tuple
x, y = coordinates
```

This feature is especially useful when working with functions that return multiple values.

5. Tuple Concatenation

Tuples can be concatenated using the + operator.

```
# Tuple concatenation
combined_coordinates = coordinates + (5, 10)
```

6. Common Tuple Operations

Tuples support operations like finding the length and checking membership.

```
# Common tuple operations
tuple_length = len(coordinates)
is_10_present = 10 in coordinates
```

Tuples are beneficial when you want to ensure that a set of values remains constant and should not be accidentally modified during program execution.

Dictionaries

Dictionaries, often referred to as dicts, are an essential data structure in Python for organizing and storing data as key-value pairs. They are particularly useful when quick lookups or mappings are required.

1. **Creating Dictionaries**

For the purpose of defining dictionaries, curly brackets are utilized, and colons are utilized for separating key-value pairs.

```
# Creating a dictionary

person = {'name': 'Alice', 'age': 25, 'city': 'Wonderland'}
```

2. **Accessing Values**

Values in a dictionary are accessed using their corresponding keys.

```
# Accessing values
person_name = person['name']
person_age = person['age']
```

Attempting to access a key that does not exist results in a **KeyError**. To avoid this, you can use the **get()** method.

```
# Using get() to access values

person_city = person.get('city', 'Unknown')
```

3. **Modifying Dictionaries**

Dictionaries are mutable, allowing you to add, modify, or remove key-value pairs.

```
# Modifying dictionaries
person['age'] = 26
person['gender'] = 'Female'
del person['city']
```

4. Common Dictionary Operations

Dictionaries support various operations, comprising checking membership, finding the number of key-value pairs, and extracting keys or values.

```python
# Common dictionary operations
is_city_present = 'city' in person
num_key_value_pairs = len(person)
person_keys = person.keys()
person_values = person.values()
```

5. Dictionary Comprehensions

The ability to generate dictionaries in a condensed form is made possible via dictionary comprehensions, which are comparable to list comprehensions.

```python
# Dictionary comprehension

squared_numbers_dict = {x: x**2 for x in range(5)}
```

This example creates a dictionary where keys are numbers from **0** to **4**, and values are their squares.

Dictionaries excel in scenarios where you need to associate values with unique keys, allowing for efficient lookup operations.

Choosing the Right Structure

Selecting the appropriate data structure is crucial for designing efficient and maintainable code. Here's a decision-making guide to help you choose the right structure for various scenarios:

Use Lists When:

- You need an ordered collection of items.
- Elements might need to be added, removed, or modified during program execution.
- Index-based access is sufficient for your use case.

Use Tuples When:

- You have a collection of values that should remain constant.
- Immutable data is required for specific use cases.
- Unpacking values is beneficial.

Use Dictionaries When:

- You need to associate values with unique keys for efficient lookups.
- Key-value pairs are a natural way to signify your data.
- Quick insertion, deletion, and lookup operations are essential.

Choosing the right data structure depends on the nature of your data and the operations you need to perform. Python's flexibility in offering multiple data structures allows you to tailor your choices to the specific requirements of your program.

2.3 - Control Flow and Decision Making in Python

In this chapter, we explore the mechanisms that allow you to control the flow of your Python programs, making decisions and executing repetitive tasks.

Understanding If-Else Statements

The Anatomy of an If Statement

At its core, an if statement in Python lets you to execute a block of code if a identified condition is true. The syntax is straightforward:

```
# Basic if statement

if condition:

    # Code to execute if the condition is true
```

Let's break down the components:

- **if keyword:** Initiates the if statement.
- **condition:** The expression that evaluates to either True or False.
- **Indented block:** The code to be executed if the condition is true. The indentation (typically four spaces) is crucial in Python to define the scope of the code block.

Instance:

```
# Instance if statement

temperature = 25


if temperature > 20:

    print("It's a warm day!")
```

In this instance, the condition **temperature > 20** is true, so the indented block containing the **print** statement is executed.

Expanding with Else

While if statements handle the case when a condition is true, you often need to account for the opposite scenario.

This is where the **else** clause comes into play.

```
# If-else statement

if condition:

    # Code to execute if the condition is true

else:

    # Code to execute if the condition is false
```

In the context of an if-else statement, if the condition is true, the code block under **if** is executed; otherwise, the code block under **else** is executed.

Instance:

```
# Instance if-else statement

temperature = 15

if temperature > 20:

    print("It's a warm day!")

else:

    print("It's a cool day.")
```

Handling Multiple Conditions

In many scenarios, you'll encounter situations where multiple conditions need to be evaluated.

The **elif** (short for "else if") clause allows you to check additional conditions after the initial **if** condition.

```
# If-elif-else statement

if condition1:

    # Code to execute if condition1 is true

elif condition2:

    # Code to execute if condition1 is false and condition2 is true

else:

    # Code to execute if both condition1 and condition2 are false
```

The **elif** clause is evaluated only if the preceding **if** or **elif** conditions are false. If any of them is true, the corresponding block is executed, and the subsequent **elif** and **else** blocks are skipped.

Instance:

```
# Instance if-elif-else statement

temperature = 25

if temperature > 30:

    print("It's a hot day!")

elif temperature > 20:

    print("It's a warm day.")
```

```
else:

    print("It's a cool day.")
```

In this instance, the first condition **temperature > 30** is false, so the program moves to the next condition. Since **temperature > 20** is true, the corresponding block is executed, and the **else** block is skipped.

Nested If-Else Statements

As your code logic becomes more intricate, you might find the need to nest if-else statements within one another. This creates a hierarchy of conditions, allowing you to handle complex decision trees.

```
# Nested if-else statements

if condition1:

    # Code to execute if condition1 is true

    if condition2:

        # Code to execute if both condition1 and condition2 are true

    else:

        # Code to execute if condition1 is true and condition2 is false

else:

    # Code to execute if condition1 is false
```

Each level of indentation signifies a deeper level of nesting. It's crucial to maintain clarity in your code when using nested if-else statements, as excessive nesting can lead to reduced readability.

Instance:

```python
# Instance nested if-else statements

age = 25

income = 50000


if age > 18:

    if income > 30000:

        print("You qualify for a loan.")

    else:

        print("Your income is too low.")

else:

    print("You must be at least 18 years old to apply for a loan.")
```

In this instance, the program first checks if the age is greater than 18. If true, it further evaluates the income condition. The code execution depends on both conditions, showcasing the flexibility of nested if-else statements.

Logical Operators

To build more sophisticated conditions, you can leverage logical operators in conjunction with if-else statements. The three main logical operators in Python are:

- **and:** Yields True when both conditions are true.
- **or:** Yields True if at least one condition is true.
- **not:** Inverts the truth value of the condition.

Instance:

```
# Logical operators in if statements
temperature = 25
humidity = 70
if temperature > 20 and humidity < 80:
    print("The weather is pleasant.")
```

Here, the condition **temperature > 20 and humidity < 80** is true, so the indented block is executed.

Ternary Operator

For simple if-else scenarios where you need to assign a value depending on a condition, Python offers a concise syntax known as the ternary operator.

```
# Ternary operator

variable = value_if_true if condition else value_if_false
```

Instance:

```
# Ternary operator example

age = 22

status = "Adult" if age >= 18 else "Minor"

print(status)
```

In this instance, the variable **status** is assigned the value "Adult" if the condition **age >= 18** is true; otherwise, it is assigned the value "Minor."

For and While Statements

The For Loop

The for loop in Python is a versatile and expressive construct designed for iterating through sequences, like lists, tuples, strings, or ranges. Its syntax is concise, making it an ideal choice when the number of iterations is known in advance.

Basic Syntax:

```python
# Basic for loop syntax

for variable in iterable:

    # Code to be executed in each iteration
```

- **for keyword:** Initiates the for loop.
- **variable:** Represents the current element in the iteration.
- **iterable:** The sequence of elements to iterate through.
- **Indented block:** The code to be executed in each iteration.

Instance: Iterating Through a List

```python
# Instance for loop iterating through a list

fruits = ['apple', 'banana', 'orange']


for fruit in fruits:

    print(fruit)
```

In this instance, the for loop iterates through the list **fruits**, and in each iteration, the variable **fruit** takes on the value of the current element. The indented block prints each fruit, resulting in the following output:

apple

banana

orange

Range Function

For loops frequently employ the range() function to produce a sequence of numbers. It has three forms:

- **range(stop):** Generates numbers from 0 to **stop - 1**.
- **range(start, stop):** Generates numbers from **start** to **stop - 1**.
- **range(start, stop, step):** Generates numbers from **start** to **stop - 1** with the identified step.

Instance: Using range() with For Loop

```
# Instance using range() with for loop

for i in range(5):

   print(i)
```

This code snippet prints numbers from 0 to 4, showcasing the simplicity and power of combining **range()** with a for loop.

Iterating Through Index and Value Pairs

In specific scenarios, you might need both the index and value of elements during iteration. The **enumerate()** function comes to the rescue, providing a concise way to achieve this.

Instance: Using enumerate() with For Loop

```
# Instance using enumerate() with for loop

fruits = ['apple', 'banana', 'orange']
```

```
for index, fruit in enumerate(fruits):

    print(f"Index: {index}, Fruit: {fruit}")
```

This code outputs:

```
Index: 0, Fruit: apple

Index: 1, Fruit: banana

Index: 2, Fruit: orange
```

List Comprehensions

List comprehensions provide a concise and expressive way to create lists. They are a form of syntactic sugar for writing a for loop that appends to a list.

Instance: List Comprehension

```
# Instance list comprehension

squared_numbers = [x**2 for x in range(5)]

print(squared_numbers)
```

This code creates a list of squared numbers from 0 to 4 in a single line, demonstrating the power and elegance of list comprehensions.

The While Loop

While loops in Python provide a various approach to iteration compared to for loops. They continue executing as long as a identified condition remains true, making them suitable for scenarios where the number of iterations is not predetermined.

Basic Syntax:

```
# Basic while loop syntax

while condition:

    # Code to be executed as long as the condition is true
```

- **while keyword:** Initiates the while loop.
- **condition:** The expression that evaluates to either True or False.
- **Indented block:** The code to be executed as long as the condition is true.

Instance: Iterating with a While Loop

```
# Instance while loop

count = 0

while count < 5:

    print(count)

    count += 1
```

In this instance, the while loop continues executing as long as the condition **count < 5** is true. The variable **count** is incremented in each iteration, resulting in the following output:

```
0

1

2

3

4
```

Infinite Loops and Break Statement

While loops have the potential to create infinite loops if not used carefully. To mitigate this risk, the **break** statement can be employed to exit the loop prematurely depending on a specific condition.

Instance: Infinite Loop with Break

```
# Instance infinite loop with break

count = 0


while True:

    print(count)

    count += 1


    if count >= 5:

        break
```

In this instance, the while loop is designed to run indefinitely (**while True**). However, the **break** statement is employed when **count** exceeds or equals 5, terminating the loop.

Else Clause with While Loop

Similar to the else clause in for loops, while loops can also have an else clause that is executed when the condition becomes false.

Instance: Else Clause with While Loop

```
# Instance else clause with while loop

count = 0

while count < 5:

    print(count)

    count += 1

else:

    print("Loop finished.")
```

In this instance, the else clause is executed when the while loop condition becomes false, providing a clear indication that the loop has finished.

Choosing Between For and While Loops

The choice between for and while loops depends on the nature of the task and the structure of the data you're working with.

Use For Loops When:

- The number of iterations is known in advance.
- You are iterating over a sequence (list, tuple, string, etc.).
- You need to perform a specific task for each item in the sequence.

Use While Loops When:

- The number of iterations is not known in advance.
- You need to iterate until a specific condition is met.
- You are dealing with scenarios where flexibility in looping conditions is crucial.

It's essential to choose the loop type that best suits the requirements of your specific task to ensure both efficiency and readability in your code.

2.4 - Deep Dive into Functions and Object-Oriented Python Programming

In this advanced chapter, we explore the intricacies of functions and delve into the principles of object-oriented programming (OOP) in Python.

Function Fundamentals

Fundamentally, a function is a structured and reusable code block designed to execute a particular task. By defining functions, you encapsulate a set of instructions, making it easier to manage, update, and reuse code throughout your program. Let's dive into the fundamental components of defining a function in Python.

Basic Syntax:

```
# Basic function syntax

def function_name(parameters):

    """

    Docstring: Description of the function.

    """

    # Code to be executed

    return result
```

- **def keyword:** Initiates the function definition.

- **function_name:** A user-defined name for the function.

- **parameters:** Input values that the function can accept (optional).

- **Docstring:** A string that offers documentation for the function (optional but highly recommended).

- **Indented block:** The code to be executed when the function is called.

- **return statement:** Specifies the value to be returned to the caller (optional).

Instance: A Simple Addition Function

```
# Instance of a simple addition function

def add_numbers(a, b):

    """

    Adds two numbers and returns the result.

    """

    result = a + b

    return result
```

In this instance, the function **add_numbers** takes two parameters (**a** and **b**), performs the addition, and returns the result.

Calling Functions

Once a function is defined, you can call or invoke it to execute the code within its block. Calling a function involves providing arguments (values for the parameters, if any) and capturing any return values.

Instance: Calling the Addition Function

```
# Calling the add_numbers function
```

```
result = add_numbers(3, 5)

print(result)
```

This code calls the **add_numbers** function with arguments **3** and **5**, captures the result, and prints it, resulting in the output **8**.

Parameters and Arguments

Parameters allow functions to receive input, making them versatile and adaptable to various scenarios. Arguments are the actual values passed to the parameters when a function is called.

Positional Arguments

In Python, arguments are matched to parameters depending on their order. These are called positional arguments.

Instance: Positional Arguments

```
# Function with positional arguments

def greet(name, greeting):

    """

    Prints a personalized greeting.

    """

    print(f"{greeting}, {name}!")


# Calling the greet function with positional arguments

greet("Alice", "Hello")
```

Here, the function **greet** has two parameters (**name** and **greeting**). When called with the arguments **"Alice"** and **"Hello"**, the output is **Hello, Alice!**.

Default Values

You can assign default values to parameters, making them optional during function calls. This offers flexibility while maintaining a sensible default behavior.

Instance: Default Values

```python
# Function with default parameter values

def greet(name, greeting="Hello"):

    """

    Prints a personalized greeting with a default value.

    """

    print(f"{greeting}, {name}!")
# Calling the greet function with and without specifying the greeting

greet("Bob")  # Output: Hello, Bob!

greet("Charlie", "Good morning")  # Output: Good morning, Charlie!
```

In this instance, the **greeting** parameter has a default value of **"Hello"**. When the function is called without specifying a greeting, it uses the default value.

Keyword Arguments

You can use keyword arguments to explicitly match values to parameters, regardless of their order. This enhances code readability and allows you to skip optional parameters.

Instance: Keyword Arguments

```python
# Function with keyword arguments

def calculate_total(price, tax_rate=0.08, discount=0):

    """

    Calculates the total price with tax and discount.

    """

    total = price + (price * tax_rate) - discount

    return total

# Calling the calculate_total function with keyword arguments

total_price = calculate_total(100, discount=10, tax_rate=0.1)

print(total_price)
```

Here, the function **calculate_total** accepts **price**, **tax_rate**, and **discount** as parameters. When calling the function, the order of keyword arguments does not matter, providing flexibility in function invocation.

Return Values

Functions can return values to the caller using the **return** statement. This enables the function to communicate results or perform actions depending on the calculated values.

Instance: Returning a List of Squares

```python
# Function that returns a list of squares

def calculate_squares(n):

    """

    Returns a list of squares from 1 to n.
```

```python
    """

    squares = [i**2 for i in range(1, n + 1)]

    return squares

# Calling the calculate_squares function

result = calculate_squares(5)

print(result)
```

In this instance, the function **calculate_squares** generates a list of squares from 1 to **n** and returns the result. The output of calling this function with **5** as an argument is **[1, 4, 9, 16, 25]**.

Multiple Return Values

A function can return multiple values as a tuple. The caller can then use tuple unpacking to capture the individual values.

Instance: Returning Multiple Values

```python
# Function that returns multiple values

def calculate_stats(numbers):

    """

    Returns the sum and average of a list of numbers.

    """

    total = sum(numbers)

    average = total / len(numbers)

    return total, average

# Calling the calculate_stats function
```

```
result_tuple = calculate_stats([10, 20, 30, 40, 50])

total_sum, average_value = result_tuple

print(f"Total: {total_sum}, Average: {average_value}")
```

In this instance, the function **calculate_stats** computes the sum and average of a list of numbers and returns both values as a tuple. The caller then unpacks the tuple into individual variables for further use.

Docstrings

Good documentation is essential for writing maintainable code. Docstrings, short for documentation strings, provide a way to document functions, explaining their purpose, parameters, and expected behavior.

Instance: Docstring for a Function

```
# Function with a docstring

def calculate_power(base, exponent):

    """

    Calculates the power of a number.


    Parameters:

    - base (float): The base number.

    - exponent (int): The exponent to which the base is raised.


    Returns:

    float: The result of base raised to the power of exponent.
```

```
    """

    result = base**exponent

    return result
```

Here, the docstring offers information about the purpose of the function, the parameters it accepts, and the type of value it returns.

Scope of Variables

Understanding variable scope is crucial when working with functions. Variables defined inside a function are considered local to that function, while variables defined outside any function are considered global.

Instance: Variable Scope

```python
# Global variable

global_var = 10


# Function with local variable

def modify_global_var():

    """

    Modifies the global variable.

    """

    local_var = 5

    global global_var

    global_var += local_var
```

```
# Calling the function

modify_global_var()

print(global_var)  # Output: 15
```

In this instance, the function **modify_global_var** modifies the global variable **global_var**. While the function has access to global variables, it's essential to use the **global** keyword when intending to modify them.

Lambda Functions

Lambda functions, also known as anonymous functions, are a concise way to define small functions without the need for a formal function definition. They are often used for short, one-time operations.

Basic Syntax:

```
# Basic lambda function syntax

lambda arguments: expression
```

Instance: Lambda Function for Squaring

```
# Lambda function for squaring

square = lambda x: x**2


# Using the lambda function

result = square(5)

print(result)  # Output: 25
```

Lambda functions are particularly useful when a small, anonymous function is needed for a specific task, like mapping or filtering elements in a list.

Embracing Object-Oriented Principles in Python

The fundamental concept behind object-oriented programming is that it is a paradigm for programming that replicates the real world by expressing entities as instances of objects. Every individual object is a representation of a class, which is a blueprint that specifies the characteristics and behaviors that are shared by all items of a particular type. OOP brings a new level of abstraction to code, allowing developers to think in terms of objects and their interactions, mirroring real-world scenarios more closely.

Key Concepts of OOP:

- **Classes:** Blueprint for objects, defining attributes (data) and methods (functions) that the objects will have.
- **Objects:** Instances of classes, representing specific entities in the program.
- **Encapsulation:** Bundling data (attributes) and methods that operate on that data within a single unit (class).
- **Inheritance:** Mechanism for creating a new class that is a modified version of an existing class, inheriting its attributes and methods.
- **Polymorphism:** The capability for objects from diverse classes to be regarded as objects of a shared superclass, facilitating code flexibility and extensibility.

Instance: Creating a Basic Class in Python

Let's start by creating a simple class to illustrate the fundamental concepts. In this instance, we'll define a **Person** class with attributes for name and age, and a method to introduce the person.

```
# Definition of the Person class

class Person:
```

```python
    def __init__(self, name, age):

        self.name = name

        self.age = age


    def introduce(self):

        print(f"Hello, my name is {self.name} and I am {self.age} years old.")


# Creating an instance of the Person class

person1 = Person("Alice", 25)


# Calling the introduce method

person1.introduce()
```

In this instance:

- The __init__ method initializes the object with the provided name and age.
- The **introduce** method prints a personalized introduction.
- An instance **person1** of the **Person** class is created, and the **introduce** method is called.

Encapsulation

There is a key idea of object-oriented programming (OOP) known as encapsulation. This principle entails combining the data (attributes) and the techniques operating on that data into a single unit known as the class. This bundling helps protect the internal state of an object and allows controlled access through methods, promoting a clear interface for interacting with objects.

Instance: Encapsulation in a Bank Account Class

Let's consider a **BankAccount** class where encapsulation ensures that the account balance is protected, and transactions are performed securely through methods.

```python
# Definition of the BankAccount class

class BankAccount:

    def __init__(self, account_holder, balance=0):

        self.account_holder = account_holder

        self.__balance = balance  # Private attribute, denoted by double underscores


    def deposit(self, amount):

        self.__balance += amount

        print(f"Deposit of ${amount} successful. New balance: ${self.__balance}")


    def withdraw(self, amount):

        if amount <= self.__balance:

            self.__balance -= amount

            print(f"Withdrawal of ${amount} successful. New balance: ${self.__balance}")

        else:

            print("Insufficient funds.")


    def get_balance(self):
```

```
        return self.__balance


# Creating an instance of the BankAccount class

account1 = BankAccount("Alice")


# Performing transactions

account1.deposit(1000)

account1.withdraw(500)

balance = account1.get_balance()

print(f"Current balance: ${balance}")
```

In this instance:

- The __**balance** attribute is private, accessible only within the class.
- The **deposit** and **withdraw** methods ensure controlled access to the balance, performing transactions securely.
- The **get_balance** method offers a read-only access point to retrieve the balance.

Encapsulation not only safeguards the internal state of objects but also contributes to code maintenance and reduces the likelihood of unintended interference.

Inheritance

Inheritance is a powerful mechanism in OOP that allows a new class to inherit attributes and methods from an existing class, creating an association among them. The behavior of the current class, which is referred to as the superclass or base class, can be extended or modified by the new class, which is more commonly referred to as a subclass or derived class.

Instance: Inheritance in a Shape Hierarchy

Consider a hierarchy of shapes, where a **Shape** class serves as the base class, and specific shapes like **Circle** and **Rectangle** inherit from it.

```python
# Definition of the Shape class (Base class)
class Shape:
    def __init__(self, color):
        self.color = color
    def area(self):
        pass  # To be implemented by subclasses
# Subclass Circle inheriting from Shape
class Circle(Shape):
    def __init__(self, color, radius):
        super().__init__(color)
        self.radius = radius
    def area(self):
        return 3.14 * self.radius**2
# Subclass Rectangle inheriting from Shape
class Rectangle(Shape):
    def __init__(self, color, length, width):
        super().__init__(color)
        self.length = length
        self.width = width
    def area(self):
        return self.length * self.width

# Creating instances of Circle and Rectangle
circle1 = Circle("Red", 5)
rectangle1 = Rectangle("Blue", 4, 6)
```

```
# Calculating and printing areas
print(f"Area of the circle: {circle1.area()} square units")
print(f"Area of the rectangle: {rectangle1.area()} square units")
```

In this instance:

- The **Shape** class defines a common attribute **color** and a method **area**, to be implemented by subclasses.
- The **Circle** and **Rectangle** classes inherit from **Shape** using the **super()** function.
- Each subclass offers its implementation of the **area** method, tailored to its specific geometry.

Inheritance promotes code reuse, allowing developers to build on existing classes and create hierarchies that reflect associations between entities in the problem domain.

Polymorphism

Polymorphism, originating from the Greek term meaning "many forms," stands as a crucial concept in Object-Oriented Programming (OOP), enabling the treatment of objects from various classes as objects of a shared superclass. This flexibility enables code to be more extensible and adaptable to diverse scenarios.

Instance: Polymorphism in a Zoo Scenario

Consider a zoo simulation where various animals, like lions and parrots, share common behavior (e.g., making sounds) but also exhibit unique characteristics.

```
# Definition of the Animal class (Base class)
class Animal:
    def __init__(self, name):
        self.name = name
    def make_sound(self):
```

```python
    pass  # To be implemented by subclasses
# Subclass Lion inheriting from Animal
class Lion(Animal):
  def make_sound(self):
    return "Roar!"
# Subclass Parrot inheriting from Animal
class Parrot(Animal):
  def make_sound(self):
    return "Squawk!"
# Creating instances of Lion and Parrot
lion1 = Lion("Leo")
parrot1 = Parrot("Polly")
# Using polymorphism to make sounds
animals = [lion1, parrot1]
for animal in animals:
  print(f"{animal.name}: {animal.make_sound()}")
```

In this instance:

- The **Animal** class defines a common attribute **name** and a method **make_sound**, to be implemented by subclasses.
- The **Lion** and **Parrot** classes inherit from **Animal** and provide their implementations of the **make_sound** method.
- The **animals** list contains instances of various subclasses, showcasing polymorphism as each object can be treated as an **Animal**.

Polymorphism simplifies code by allowing a single interface (**make_sound** in this case) to be used with objects of various types, providing flexibility and reducing code duplication.

Classes and Objects

Before delving into the specifics of classes and objects, let's grasp the essence of why they are crucial in the context of object-oriented programming.

Abstraction and Modeling

OOP is rooted in the idea of modeling real-world entities and their interactions within a program. Classes act as blueprints, defining the properties (attributes) and behaviors (methods) that objects of that class will exhibit. Objects, on the other hand, are instances of these classes, representing tangible entities within the program.

Modularity and Reusability

Classes promote modularity by encapsulating related functionality into a single unit. This modularity enhances code organization, making it more readable and maintainable. Moreover, the reusability aspect of OOP allows developers to instantiate and use objects depending on existing class definitions, reducing redundancy and promoting efficient code reuse.

Encapsulation for Data Security

Encapsulation, a key principle of OOP, involves bundling data and methods that operate on that data within a single unit—the class. This bundling not only promotes code organization but also safeguards the internal state of objects. Access to the internal state is controlled through methods, enhancing data security and preventing unintended interference.

Relationships and Inheritance

Classes can be hierarchically organized through inheritance, where a new class (subclass) can inherit attributes and methods from an existing class (superclass). This association fosters code reuse and allows developers to create specialized classes that build upon the functionality of more general classes.

Defining Classes in Python

In Python, defining a class involves specifying its attributes and methods. Let's start with a simple example of a **Car** class.

Instance: Defining a Car Class

```python
class Car:

    def __init__(self, make, model, year):

        self.make = make

        self.model = model

        self.year = year


    def display_info(self):

        print(f"{self.year} {self.make} {self.model}")
```

In this instance:

- The **__init__** method is a special method known as the constructor. It is called when an object is created and initializes the object's attributes.
- The **display_info** method prints information about the car.

To create an instance of the **Car** class, we instantiate it as follows:

```python
my_car = Car("Toyota", "Camry", 2022)
```

Here, **my_car** is an object (instance) of the **Car** class. The attributes (**make**, **model**, and **year**) are specific to this instance.

Creating Object Instances

Creating object instances involves using the class as a template to instantiate specific objects.

Each instance has its own set of attributes and can invoke the methods defined in its class.

Instance: Creating Multiple Car Instances

```python
car1 = Car("Honda", "Civic", 2023)

car2 = Car("Ford", "Mustang", 2022)

car3 = Car("Chevrolet", "Malibu", 2021)

# Calling the display_info method for each car

car1.display_info()  # Output: 2023 Honda Civic

car2.display_info()  # Output: 2022 Ford Mustang

car3.display_info()  # Output: 2021 Chevrolet Malibu
```

In this instance, we create three instances of the **Car** class—**car1**, **car2**, and **car3**. Each instance represents a specific car with its own attributes (**make**, **model**, and **year**).

Attributes and Methods

Attributes are the properties of a class that store data, while methods are functions associated with the class that define its behavior. Let's explore these concepts further.

Attributes

Attributes are defined within the constructor (**__init__**) and are specific to each instance of the class.

```python
class Dog:

  def __init__(self, name, breed):

    self.name = name
```

```
    self.breed = breed
```

In this instance, the **Dog** class has attributes **name** and **breed**. To create a **Dog** instance:

```
my_dog = Dog("Buddy", "Golden Retriever")

print(my_dog.name)  # Output: Buddy

print(my_dog.breed)  # Output: Golden Retriever
```

Methods

Methods define the behavior of a class and are invoked on instances of the class.

```
class Circle:

    def __init__(self, radius):

        self.radius = radius


    def calculate_area(self):

        return 3.14 * self.radius**2
```

Here, the **Circle** class has a method **calculate_area** that computes the area of the circle. To use this method:

```
my_circle = Circle(5)

area = my_circle.calculate_area()

print(area)  # Output: 78.5
```

Methods can also take parameters and operate on the attributes of the instance.

Constructors and Destructors

Constructors (__init__)

The **__init__** method serves as a special function within Python classes, getting invoked upon the creation of an object. It initializes the attributes of the object. Let's revisit the **Car** class:

```python
class Car:

    def __init__(self, make, model, year):

        self.make = make

        self.model = model

        self.year = year
```

When we create an instance of this class, the constructor is automatically called:

```python
my_car = Car("Toyota", "Camry", 2022)
```

The values **"Toyota"**, **"Camry"**, and **2022** are passed as arguments to the constructor, initializing the attributes **make**, **model**, and **year**.

Destructors (__del__)

While the constructor initializes objects, a destructor (**__del__**) can be used to perform cleanup operations prior to an object is destroyed. It's essential to note that the use of destructors is less common in Python, as the garbage collector automatically reclaims memory.

```python
class MyClass:

    def __init__(self):

        print("Object initialized.")
```

```python
    def __del__(self):

        print("Object destroyed.")

obj = MyClass()

# Output: Object initialized.

del obj

# Output: Object destroyed.
```

Inheritance

A key notion in object-oriented programming (OOP) is called inheritance, and it enables a new class, known as a subclass, to take on characteristics and functions from a prior class, known as a superclass. This mechanism promotes code reuse and the creation of specialized classes.

Instance: Inheritance in a Vehicle Hierarchy

Let's extend our understanding by introducing a **Vehicle** superclass and deriving **Car** and **Motorcycle** subclasses:

```python
class Vehicle:

    def __init__(self, make, model, year):

        self.make = make

        self.model = model

        self.year = year


    def display_info(self):

        print(f"{self.year} {self.make} {self.model}")
```

118

```python
class Car(Vehicle):

    def drive(self):

        print("Driving a car.")


class Motorcycle(Vehicle):

    def ride(self):

        print("Riding a motorcycle.")
```

Here, the **Car** and **Motorcycle** classes inherit from the **Vehicle** class. They not only have their specialized methods (**drive** and **ride**) but also inherit the **display_info** method from the **Vehicle** class.

```python
car = Car("Toyota", "Camry", 2022)

car.display_info()  # Output: 2022 Toyota Camry

car.drive()  # Output: Driving a car.


motorcycle = Motorcycle("Harley-Davidson", "Sportster", 2021)

motorcycle.display_info()  # Output: 2021 Harley-Davidson Sportster

motorcycle.ride()  # Output: Riding a motorcycle.
```

In this instance, instances of both **Car** and **Motorcycle** can access the common **display_info** method from the **Vehicle** class, showcasing the power of inheritance in creating hierarchical associations.

Polymorphism

Polymorphism, denoting "many forms," is a fundamental principle in Object-Oriented Programming (OOP) that facilitates the treatment of objects from distinct classes as if they were objects of a shared superclass. This flexibility enhances code adaptability and readability.

Instance: Polymorphism in a Zoo Scenario

Consider a zoo simulation where various animals share common behavior, like making sounds:

```python
class Animal:
    def __init__(self, name):
        self.name = name
    def make_sound(self):
        pass  # To be implemented by subclasses
class Lion(Animal):
    def make_sound(self):
        return "Roar!"
class Parrot(Animal):
    def make_sound(self):
        return "Squawk!"
```

In this instance, both **Lion** and **Parrot** inherit from the common superclass **Animal**. Instances of these subclasses can be treated as instances of the superclass:

```python
lion = Lion("Leo")

parrot = Parrot("Polly")


# Using polymorphism to make sounds

animals = [lion, parrot]


for animal in animals:

    print(f"{animal.name}: {animal.make_sound()}")
```

The output demonstrates how objects of various classes, each implementing the **make_sound** method, can be seamlessly used in a polymorphic manner.

BOOK 3: INTRODUCTION TO SQL AND DATABASE MANAGEMENT

3.1 - Introduction to Databases and SQL

Embark on a journey into the world of databases and Structured Query Language (SQL). This chapter lays the foundation for understanding the core concepts and functionalities that underpin database management.

Database Fundamentals

At its essence, a database is a structured collection of data organized to facilitate efficient retrieval and manipulation. Imagine it as a digital repository that stores information in a way that allows for easy access and management. Databases serve as a central hub for applications, enabling them to store, retrieve, and update data seamlessly.

Key Components of Databases:

1. **Tables:** Databases organize data into tables, each resembling a spreadsheet with rows and columns. Tables are used to signify entities (e.g., customers, products) and their attributes.

2. **Rows:** Also known as records or tuples, rows signify individual entries in a table. Each row contains data related to a specific entity, with each column capturing a various attribute.

3. **Columns:** Columns, or fields, define the attributes of the entities signified in a table. For instance, in a table of employees, columns might comprise "Name," "Age," and "Salary."

4. **Keys:** Keys are crucial for starting associations between tables. A primary key uniquely recognizes each row in a table, while a foreign key links a row in one table to a corresponding row in another.

Types of Databases:

1. **Relational Databases (RDBMS):** Relational databases organize data into tables with predefined associations. Instances comprise MySQL, PostgreSQL, and Oracle Database. They adhere to the principles of the relational model, ensuring data integrity and consistency.

2. **NoSQL Databases:** NoSQL databases deviate from the structured nature of relational databases and accommodate various data models, comprising document-oriented, key-value, graph, and column-family stores. MongoDB and Cassandra are popular examples.

3. **Graph Databases:** Graph databases are tailored for managing data characterized by intricate associations, employing graph structures comprising nodes, edges, and associated properties. Neo4j is a notable example, excelling in scenarios where associations are as crucial as the data itself.

4. **In-Memory Databases:** These databases store data in the system's main memory (RAM) rather than on disk, resulting in faster data access. Redis and Apache Ignite are examples frequently used for caching and real-time analytics.

5. **Document-Oriented Databases:** MongoDB and CouchDB fall into this category, where data is stored as documents (e.g., JSON or BSON). These databases are adept at handling unstructured or semi-structured data.

Relational Databases

Relational databases, characterized by their structured and tabular nature, have been a cornerstone of data management for decades. Let's delve deeper into their key features and functionalities.

Normalization

Normalization is a crucial process in relational databases that minimizes data redundancy and dependency, ensuring data integrity and consistency.

This involves organizing tables to reduce duplication and dependence on individual attributes. Normal forms, like the first normal form (1NF) and third normal form (3NF), guide the normalization process.

Transactions

Relational databases adhere to the ACID properties (Atomicity, Consistency, Isolation, Durability) to guarantee the reliability of transactions:

1. **Atomicity:** Transactions are handled as if they were indivisible units, which guarantees that either every one of the operations contained in a transaction are finished or zero of them are finished.

2. **Consistency:** Databases are brought from one legitimate state to another through the process of transactions, which ensures that data is consistent.

3. **Isolation:** Transactions are carried out independently of one another, which eliminates the possibility of mutual intervention.

4. **Durability:** This refers to the fact that once a transaction commits itself, the modifications it makes are irreversible and can withstand future system failures.

Indexing

Indexing is a method employed to boost the efficiency of data retrieval processes within a database. By starting an index on one or multiple columns, the database system can rapidly pinpoint and retrieve the rows linked to specific values in those columns. Efficient indexing significantly improves query performance, especially in large datasets.

NoSQL Databases

As data requirements evolved, the limitations of relational databases became apparent in handling large volumes of unstructured or semi-structured data. NoSQL databases emerged as a response to these challenges, offering flexibility and scalability.

Document-Oriented Databases

MongoDB, a popular document-oriented database, stores data in flexible, JSON-like documents. Each document can have a various structure, allowing for dynamic schema design. This flexibility is advantageous when dealing with data that doesn't fit neatly into tables.

Key-Value Stores

Key-value stores, exemplified by databases like Redis and Amazon DynamoDB, store data as key-value pairs. These databases are efficient for scenarios where simple data retrieval and storage are paramount.

Column-Family Stores

Databases like Apache Cassandra organize data into columns rather than rows, making them suitable for scenarios where rapid write and retrieval of large amounts of data are essential.

Graph Databases

Neo4j, a prominent graph database, is optimized for handling data with intricate associations. It leverages graph structures to signify and navigate associations between data points efficiently.

Choosing the Right Database

The selection of a database system depends on various factors, comprising the nature of the data, scalability requirements, and the complexity of associations.

While relational databases excel in maintaining data integrity through structured data, NoSQL databases offer flexibility and scalability for diverse data models.

Considerations for Choosing a Database:

1. **Data Model:** Understand the nature of your data—structured, semi-structured, or unstructured. Choose a database that aligns with your data model.

2. **Scalability:** Consider the scalability requirements of your application. NoSQL databases often provide better scalability options for distributed and horizontally scalable architectures.

3. **Consistency vs. Flexibility:** Relational databases prioritize data consistency, making them suitable for applications with strict data integrity requirements. NoSQL databases, on the other hand, prioritize flexibility and scalability.

4. **Query Complexity:** If your application involves complex queries and transactions, a relational database might be more suitable. For simpler queries and high-speed data retrieval, NoSQL databases can be advantageous.

The Role of SQL

SQL traces its roots back to the early 1970s when IBM researchers Donald D. Chamberlin and Raymond F. Boyce developed a language for managing and manipulating databases.

Initially known as SEQUEL (Structured English Query Language), it aimed to provide a user-friendly and English-like interface for interacting with databases.

In the subsequent years, SQL evolved as an industry standard, with contributions from various organizations and database vendors.

The American National Standards Institute (ANSI) and the International Organization for Standardization (ISO) have played pivotal roles in standardizing SQL, ensuring its widespread adoption and interoperability across diverse database management systems.

Essential Components of SQL

SQL is designed as a domain-specific language that facilitates the interaction with relational databases. Its syntax is characterized by a series of declarative statements that convey the desired operations on the database. Let's explore the essential components that form the building blocks of SQL.

Data Definition Language (DDL)

The Data Definition Language (DDL) in SQL is concerned with the definition and modification of database structures. Key DDL statements comprise:

1. **CREATE:** This statement creates database objects like tables, indexes, and views.

```
CREATE TABLE employees (

    employee_id INT PRIMARY KEY,

    first_name VARCHAR(50),

    last_name VARCHAR(50),

    department_id INT

);
```

2. **ALTER:** The ALTER statement is employed for modifying existing database objects, like adding or removing columns.

```
ALTER TABLE employees

ADD COLUMN email VARCHAR(100);
```

3. **DROP:** DROP is utilized to remove database objects like tables or indexes.

```
DROP TABLE employees;
```

3.2 - Foundational SQL Commands and Techniques

In this chapter, we dive into foundational SQL commands and techniques, equipping you with the skills needed to interact with and manipulate data in a relational database.

SELECT, FROM, WHERE

At the heart of SQL lies the SELECT statement, a versatile command that forms the cornerstone of querying databases. It allows users to retrieve specific columns or expressions from one or more tables, offering a tailored view of the data. The syntax of the SELECT statement is elegantly straightforward:

```
SELECT column1, column2, ...

FROM table_name;
```

Basic Usage of SELECT

The basic usage involves specifying the columns to be retrieved from a particular table. For example:

```
SELECT first_name, last_name

FROM employees;
```

This query retrieves the first name and last name of all employees from the "employees" table. The SELECT statement empowers users to choose precisely which columns are relevant to their query, avoiding the retrieval of unnecessary data.

Wildcard (*) in SELECT

For scenarios where all columns need to be retrieved, the wildcard (*) can be employed:

```
SELECT *
```

```
FROM products;
```

This query fetches all columns from the "products" table. While convenient, using the wildcard should be done judiciously, as it may lead to the retrieval of more data than necessary, potentially impacting performance.

Using Expressions in SELECT

The SELECT statement also allows for the inclusion of expressions, enabling users to perform calculations or concatenate strings during data retrieval:

```
SELECT product_name, price, price * 0.9 AS discounted_price

FROM products;
```

In this instance, an expression calculates the discounted price by applying a 10% discount to the original price.

The FROM Clause

While the SELECT statement determines the columns to be retrieved, the FROM clause specifies the source of the data. It recognizes the tables from which the data will be queried, forming the foundation for a well-structured SQL query:

```
SELECT column1, column2, ...

FROM table1

JOIN table2 ON table1.column = table2.column;
```

Basic Usage of FROM

In its simplest form, the FROM clause recognizes the primary table from which data is to be retrieved:

```
SELECT product_name, price

FROM products;
```

This query retrieves the product name and price columns from the "products" table.

Joining Tables with FROM

To enrich queries and retrieve data from multiple tables, the JOIN operation is utilized within the FROM clause. It establishes associations between tables depending on common columns:

SELECT employees.first_name, employees.last_name, departments.department_name

FROM employees

JOIN departments ON employees.department_id = departments.department_id;

This query joins the "employees" and "departments" tables, retrieving the first name and last name of employees along with their corresponding department names.

The WHERE Clause

While the SELECT statement and FROM clause lay the groundwork for data retrieval, the WHERE clause adds a layer of specificity by allowing users to filter data depending on identified conditions. This ensures that only relevant records are included in the result set:

SELECT column1, column2, ...

FROM table_name

WHERE condition;

Basic Usage of WHERE

The WHERE clause is integral for refining queries. For instance:

SELECT product_name, price

FROM products

WHERE category = 'Electronics' AND price > 500;

This query retrieves the product name and price of electronic products with a price exceeding 500. The WHERE clause serves as a powerful tool for tailoring results depending on specific criteria.

Filtering with Comparison Operators

The WHERE clause supports various comparison operators, like = (equal to), <> or != (not equal to), < (less than), > (greater than), <= (less than or equal to), and >= (greater than or equal to). For example:

```
SELECT employee_id, first_name, last_name

FROM employees

WHERE department_id = 1 AND salary > 50000;
```

This query retrieves the employee ID, first name, and last name of employees in the department with ID 1 and a salary greater than 50,000.

Logical Operators in WHERE

Logical operators, comprising AND, OR, and NOT, enhance the filtering capabilities of the WHERE clause. They enable users to construct complex conditions for more nuanced data retrieval:

```
SELECT product_name, price

FROM products

WHERE (category = 'Electronics' OR category = 'Appliances') AND price > 200;
```

In this instance, the query retrieves product names and prices for items in the 'Electronics' or 'Appliances' category with a price exceeding 200.

Combining SELECT, FROM, and WHERE

The true power of SQL unfolds when these fundamental components—SELECT, FROM, and WHERE—are combined strategically to craft precise queries tailored to specific informational needs. Consider the following example:

```
SELECT customer_name, order_date, total_amount

FROM customers

JOIN orders ON customers.customer_id = orders.customer_id

WHERE total_amount > 1000

ORDER BY order_date DESC;
```

This query retrieves the customer name, order date, and total amount from customers who have made orders exceeding 1000, ordered by date in descending order.

This showcases the seamless integration of SELECT, FROM, and WHERE to obtain highly targeted results.

Sorting and Filtering

ORDER BY

The ORDER BY clause in SQL is a versatile command that enables the sorting of query results depending on identified columns, either in ascending (ASC) or descending (DESC) order. This functionality is crucial for presenting data in a manner that aligns with the user's informational needs.

Basic Usage of ORDER BY

The basic syntax of ORDER BY is elegantly simple:

```
SELECT column1, column2, ...
```

```
FROM table_name

ORDER BY column1 [ASC | DESC], column2 [ASC | DESC], ...;
```

For example:

```
SELECT product_name, price

FROM products

ORDER BY price DESC;
```

This query retrieves the product names and prices from the "products" table, presenting them in descending order of price. The DESC keyword indicates a descending sort, while ASC (ascending) is the default if not identified.

Sorting by Multiple Columns

ORDER BY allows for sorting by multiple columns, providing a hierarchical arrangement. Consider the following:

```
SELECT product_name, category, price

FROM products

ORDER BY category ASC, price DESC;
```

In this case, the results are first sorted alphabetically by category in ascending order, and within each category, the prices are arranged in descending order.

Sorting by Expressions

The power of ORDER BY extends to sorting by expressions, not just column values. This is particularly useful when calculations or manipulations are involved:

```
SELECT product_name, price, price * 0.9 AS discounted_price

FROM products
```

```
ORDER BY discounted_price DESC;
```

Here, the query sorts the results depending on the calculated discounted price in descending order.

NULL Values in ORDER BY

Handling NULL values requires careful consideration.

By default, NULL values are sorted at the end when using ORDER BY. For instance:

```
SELECT product_name, price

FROM products

ORDER BY price;
```

This query sorts products by price in ascending order, with NULL values positioned at the end.

GROUP BY

The GROUP BY clause is a pivotal element for aggregating data depending on specific columns, providing a concise summary of information.

It allows users to group rows that share common values in one or more columns and apply aggregate functions to the grouped data.

Basic Usage of GROUP BY

The fundamental syntax of GROUP BY is as follows:

```
SELECT column1, aggregate_function(column2), ...

FROM table_name

GROUP BY column1;
```

For example:

```
SELECT department_id, AVG(salary) as average_salary

FROM employees

GROUP BY department_id;
```

This query groups employees by department and calculates the average salary for each department.

Aggregating Functions with GROUP BY

GROUP BY is often paired with aggregate functions like COUNT, SUM, AVG, MIN, and MAX to derive meaningful insights from grouped data. Consider the following examples:

```
SELECT category, COUNT(*) as product_count

FROM products

GROUP BY category;
```

Here, the query counts the number of products in each category.

```
SELECT department_id, MAX(salary) as highest_salary

FROM employees

GROUP BY department_id;
```

This query recognizes the highest salary in each department.

Filtering GROUP BY Results with HAVING

While the WHERE clause filters rows prior to grouping, the HAVING clause filters groups after the grouping has occurred. It allows for conditions depending on aggregate values:

```
SELECT department_id, AVG(salary) as average_salary

FROM employees
```

```
GROUP BY department_id

HAVING AVG(salary) > 60000;
```

This query retrieves departments with an average salary exceeding 60,000.

GROUP BY with Multiple Columns

GROUP BY is not limited to a single column; it can be applied to multiple columns to create more granular groups:

```
SELECT department_id, job_id, AVG(salary) as average_salary

FROM employees

GROUP BY department_id, job_id;
```

This query calculates the average salary for each combination of department and job.

Sorting GROUP BY Results with ORDER BY

ORDER BY can be combined with GROUP BY to sort the results depending on aggregated values:

```
SELECT department_id, AVG(salary) as average_salary

FROM employees

GROUP BY department_id

ORDER BY average_salary DESC;
```

This query orders departments by the average salary in descending order.

Combining ORDER BY and GROUP BY

The true power of these clauses unfolds when they are combined to craft comprehensive queries that not only aggregate data but also present it in a structured and sorted manner. Consider the following example:

```sql
SELECT department_id, job_id, AVG(salary) as average_salary

FROM employees

GROUP BY department_id, job_id

HAVING AVG(salary) > 50000

ORDER BY department_id, average_salary DESC;
```

In this query, employees are grouped by department and job, but only those with an average salary exceeding 50,000 are included. The results are then ordered first by department and then by average salary in descending order.

INSERT, UPDATE, DELETE Operations

INSERT Statement

The INSERT statement is a cornerstone of SQL, allowing you to add new records to a table. This operation is essential for incorporating fresh data into your database, whether it's from user input, external sources, or generated within your application.

Basic Usage of INSERT

The basic syntax of the INSERT statement is straightforward:

```sql
INSERT INTO table_name (column1, column2, column3, ...)

VALUES (value1, value2, value3, ...);
```

For example:

```sql
INSERT INTO employees (first_name, last_name, job_id, salary)

VALUES ('John', 'Doe', 'IT_PROG', 60000);
```

This query adds a new employee record with the identified values for the first name, last name, job ID, and salary into the "employees" table.

Inserting Multiple Rows at Once

The flexibility of the INSERT statement extends to inserting multiple rows in a single query:

```
INSERT INTO employees (first_name, last_name, job_id, salary)

VALUES

  ('Alice', 'Smith', 'HR_REP', 55000),

  ('Bob', 'Jones', 'SA_REP', 70000),

  ('Eva', 'Brown', 'IT_PROG', 65000);
```

This query inserts three new records into the "employees" table simultaneously.

Inserting Data from Another Table

You can also populate a table with data from another table using the INSERT INTO ... SELECT statement:

```
INSERT INTO employees_audit

SELECT * FROM employees

WHERE hire_date > '2023-01-01';
```

This query inserts records into the "employees_audit" table depending on a condition from the "employees" table.

UPDATE Statement

The UPDATE statement empowers you to modify existing records within a table. This operation is crucial for keeping your data accurate as it evolves over time.

Basic Usage of UPDATE

The basic structure of the UPDATE statement is outlined below:

```
UPDATE table_name

SET column1 = value1, column2 = value2, ...

WHERE condition;
```

For example:

```
UPDATE employees

SET salary = salary * 1.1

WHERE department_id = 1;
```

This query increases the salary of employees in department 1 by 10%.

Updating Data Based on Another Table

You can leverage subqueries within the UPDATE statement to modify data depending on information from another table:

```
UPDATE products

SET stock_quantity = stock_quantity - order_items.quantity

FROM order_items

WHERE products.product_id = order_items.product_id

  AND order_items.order_status = 'Shipped';
```

This query adjusts the stock quantity of products depending on shipped order items.

Updating with Conditional Logic

The UPDATE statement supports conditional logic, allowing you to modify data depending on complex conditions:

```
UPDATE employees
```

```
SET bonus = CASE

    WHEN salary > 80000 THEN salary * 0.1

    WHEN salary > 60000 THEN salary * 0.07

    ELSE salary * 0.05

END;
```

This query calculates and updates the bonus for employees depending on their salary.

DELETE Statement

The DELETE statement enables you to remove records from a table, eliminating unnecessary or outdated information.

Basic Usage of DELETE

The basic structure of the DELETE statement is outlined below:

```
DELETE FROM table_name

WHERE condition;
```

For example:

```
DELETE FROM employees

WHERE department_id = 5;
```

This query removes all employees from department 5.

Deleting All Rows from a Table

To remove all rows from a table, you can use the DELETE statement without a WHERE clause:

```
DELETE FROM employees_audit;
```

This query deletes all records from the "employees_audit" table.

Deleting Data Based on Another Table

Similar to the UPDATE statement, the DELETE statement can utilize subqueries for more precise deletions:

```
DELETE FROM products

WHERE product_id IN (SELECT product_id FROM obsolete_products);
```

This query deletes products that are marked as obsolete in the "obsolete_products" table.

Combining Manipulation Operations

The true power of data manipulation in SQL unfolds when you combine these operations to craft comprehensive changes to your database. Consider the following example:

```
-- Add a new employee

INSERT INTO employees (first_name, last_name, job_id, salary)

VALUES ('Grace', 'Williams', 'SA_REP', 75000);


-- Update the department for the new employee

UPDATE employees

SET department_id = 2

WHERE first_name = 'Grace' AND last_name = 'Williams';


-- Delete obsolete data
```

```
DELETE FROM employees

WHERE hire_date < '2022-01-01';
```

In this sequence of queries, a new employee is added, their department is updated, and obsolete employee records are removed, showcasing the seamless integration of INSERT, UPDATE, and DELETE statements.

3.3 - SQL Servers and Interfaces

In this chapter, we expand your understanding of SQL by exploring SQL servers and various user interfaces, essential components for effective database management.

Exploring SQL Servers

SQL server is a database management system that employs the Structured Query Language (SQL) for interacting with databases. The server-side aspect comes into play as these systems are designed to run on a server, facilitating the management of databases, user access, and data integrity. The server acts as the central hub, handling requests, executing queries, and ensuring the seamless flow of information between the database and the applications that interact with it.

Types of SQL Servers

Local SQL Servers

Local SQL servers, often referred to as on-premises servers, are installed and run on the same physical hardware as the applications they serve. They have been a traditional choice for organizations that prioritize having direct control over their infrastructure. Two prominent examples of local SQL servers are Microsoft SQL Server and PostgreSQL.

1. **Microsoft SQL Server:** Microsoft SQL Server stands as one of the most widely used local SQL servers. Developed by Microsoft, it boasts a robust set of features, comprising support for transaction processing, business intelligence, and analytics. Its integration with the Microsoft ecosystem makes it a preferred choice for organizations heavily invested in Microsoft technologies.

2. **PostgreSQL:** PostgreSQL, an open-source relational database management system, is known for its extensibility and compliance with SQL standards. With features like support for complex data types, indexing, and advanced querying capabilities,

PostgreSQL is embraced by developers seeking a powerful and flexible local SQL server solution.

Cloud-Based SQL Servers

In the era of cloud computing, organizations increasingly turn to cloud-based SQL servers for their scalability, flexibility, and ease of management. Cloud providers offer managed database services that handle infrastructure maintenance, updates, and backups, allowing teams to focus more on application development. Two prominent cloud-based SQL servers are Amazon Aurora and Microsoft Azure SQL Database.

1. **Amazon Aurora:** Amazon Aurora, a fully managed relational database service by Amazon Web Services (AWS), is designed for high performance and availability. Compatible with MySQL and PostgreSQL, Aurora offers the benefits of both worlds— open-source compatibility and the robustness of a cloud-native solution. It automatically replicates data across multiple Availability Zones, ensuring durability and fault tolerance.

2. **Microsoft Azure SQL Database:** Azure SQL Database is a cloud-based relational database service offered by Microsoft Azure. It allows organizations to scale resources depending on demand, and its compatibility with on-premises SQL Server simplifies migration efforts. With features like automatic tuning and threat detection, Azure SQL Database offers a secure and intelligent database solution in the cloud.

Roles and Features of SQL Servers

Roles

SQL servers serve various roles in the ecosystem of database management, each contributing to the overall efficiency and functionality of the system. Some key roles comprise:

1. **Data Storage and Retrieval:** SQL servers store and organize data efficiently, providing mechanisms for rapid retrieval through structured queries.

2. **Concurrency Control:** To ensure data integrity in multi-user environments, SQL servers implement concurrency control mechanisms, allowing multiple users to access and modify data concurrently without conflicts.

3. **Security Management:** SQL servers enforce security measures to control access to databases and protect sensitive information. This includes user authentication, authorization, and encryption of data in transit and at rest.

4. **Backup and Recovery:** Robust SQL servers facilitate regular backups and offer recovery mechanisms to safeguard against data loss due to hardware failures, human errors, or other unforeseen events.

Features

The features of SQL servers vary depending on the specific implementation, but there are common functionalities that contribute to their effectiveness:

1. **Query Optimization:** SQL servers employ query optimization techniques to enhance the performance of queries. This involves choosing the most efficient execution plan depending on factors like indexes, statistics, and available resources.

2. **Transaction Management:** SQL servers ensure the atomicity, consistency, isolation, and durability (ACID) properties of transactions. This ensures that database transactions are reliable and maintain data integrity.

3. **Indexing:** Indexes are crucial for efficient data retrieval. SQL servers use indexes to quickly locate and access the rows that satisfy the conditions identified in queries, minimizing the time required for data retrieval.

4. **Stored Procedures and Triggers:** SQL servers support the creation of stored procedures—precompiled executable code that can be invoked by applications.

Triggers, on the other hand, are special types of stored procedures that automatically respond to specific events, like data modifications.

5. **Replication:** Replication allows SQL servers to create and maintain copies of databases across multiple servers. This enhances availability, fault tolerance, and load balancing.

Challenges and Considerations in SQL Server Management

While SQL servers offer powerful solutions for database management, specific challenges and considerations should be taken into account:

1. **Scalability:** Choosing a SQL server that scales effectively with the growth of data and user demand is crucial. Cloud-based solutions often provide better scalability options than traditional on-premises servers.

2. **Cost Considerations:** Cloud-based SQL servers operate on a pay-as-you-go model, where costs are incurred depending on usage. Understanding the pricing structure and optimizing resource utilization is essential to manage costs effectively.

3. **Security:** Ensuring the security of sensitive data is paramount. SQL servers must be configured with robust security measures, comprising encryption, access controls, and regular security audits.

4. **Backup and Recovery Planning:** Establishing thorough backup and recovery plans is essential to mitigate the risks associated with data loss. Regularly testing these plans ensures the ability to recover data in case of unexpected incidents.

5. **Compatibility and Integration:** Compatibility with existing systems and integration capabilities with development frameworks and tools should be considered when selecting an SQL server solution.

User Interfaces for SQL

The Command-Line Interface (CLI)

SQL interaction lies the command-line interface (CLI), a text-based interface that allows users to input commands directly. While it might seem intimidating to newcomers, the CLI offers a direct and efficient way for seasoned users to interact with databases. Let's explore two prominent CLI tools for SQL: MySQL and PostgreSQL.

MySQL CLI

MySQL, a widely used relational database management system, offers a powerful command-line interface (CLI) for engaging with databases. Individuals have the capability to establish a connection to a MySQL server and run SQL commands directly through the command line. The process typically involves entering the MySQL CLI, specifying connection details, and then executing SQL queries.

```
mysql -u username -p
```

This command initiates the MySQL CLI, prompting the user to enter their password. Once connected, users can seamlessly execute SQL commands and queries.

PostgreSQL CLI

Similar to MySQL, PostgreSQL, an open-source relational database management system, offers a powerful CLI for SQL interactions. Users can connect to a PostgreSQL server and execute queries directly from the command line.

```
psql -U username -d database_name
```

This command establishes a connection to a PostgreSQL database, allowing users to input SQL commands for execution. The PostgreSQL CLI offers a straightforward and efficient way to manage databases for those comfortable with text-based interfaces.

Graphical User Interfaces (GUIs)

For those who prefer a more visual and intuitive experience, graphical user interfaces (GUIs) for SQL databases offer an attractive alternative. These tools provide a visual representation of database structures, allowing users to interact with tables, execute queries, and manage data through point-and-click actions. Let's explore two widely used GUI tools: DBeaver and Microsoft SQL Server Management Studio (SSMS).

DBeaver

DBeaver is a versatile and open-source database tool that supports various database management systems, comprising MySQL, PostgreSQL, and SQLite. Its GUI offers an organized and user-friendly environment for SQL interactions. Users can establish connections to multiple databases, visualize schema structures, and execute SQL queries with ease.

DBeaver's multi-database support makes it a valuable tool for developers and database administrators working with diverse database systems. Its intuitive interface simplifies the process of executing SQL commands, making it accessible for users across various experience levels.

Microsoft SQL Server Management Studio (SSMS)

For those working with Microsoft SQL Server, SQL Server Management Studio (SSMS) serves as the go-to GUI tool. SSMS offers a comprehensive environment for managing SQL Server databases, offering features like query editing, visualizing database structures, and performance monitoring.

With SSMS, users can connect to SQL Server instances, create and modify databases, and execute T-SQL queries using an interactive query editor. Its integration with other Microsoft tools and services makes it a preferred choice for those immersed in the Microsoft ecosystem.

Web-Based Interfaces

In the era of cloud computing and remote work, web-based interfaces for SQL databases have gained prominence. These interfaces allow users to interact with databases using a web browser, providing the flexibility to manage databases from anywhere with internet access. Let's explore two notable web-based SQL interfaces: phpMyAdmin and Azure Data Studio.

phpMyAdmin

phpMyAdmin is a web-based tool designed for managing MySQL and MariaDB databases. It offers a user-friendly interface accessible through a web browser. Users can perform tasks like executing SQL queries, importing and exporting data, and managing database structures through an intuitive and visually appealing dashboard.

phpMyAdmin simplifies database management for users who prefer a web-based approach, allowing them to perform various actions without the need for a dedicated CLI or GUI tool.

Azure Data Studio

Azure Data Studio is a cross-platform database tool developed by Microsoft. While it can be installed locally, its web-based component, Azure Data Studio Notebooks, enables users to interact with databases through a browser. This web-based interface supports SQL Server, PostgreSQL, and MySQL.

Azure Data Studio's web-based component offers a collaborative environment where users can execute queries, visualize results, and share insights with team members. Its versatility makes it a valuable tool for those working across various database systems.

BOOK 4: ADVANCED SQL AND INTEGRATIVE TECHNIQUES

4.1 - Advanced SQL Concepts and Procedures

In this chapter, we delve into advanced SQL concepts and procedures, unlocking the full potential of SQL for sophisticated data management.

Stored Procedures

A stored procedure is a set of SQL statements that are pre-compiled and stored on the database server for subsequent execution. These procedures can accept parameters, perform operations, and return results, providing a reusable and efficient means of interacting with databases. Stored procedures offer several advantages, making them an essential component in the toolkit of any database developer or administrator.

Key Features of Stored Procedures:

1. **Encapsulation of Logic:** Stored procedures enable the encapsulation of complex business logic on the database server. This promotes a modular and organized approach to coding, enhancing code readability and maintainability.

2. **Enhanced Security:** By executing SQL queries within stored procedures, security measures can be implemented to control access and permissions. This reduces the risk of SQL injection attacks and ensures that only authorized users can interact with specific procedures.

3. **Improved Performance:** When contrasted with SQL statements that are produced dynamically, stored processes are pre-compiled and stored on the server, which results in enhanced efficiency. The execution strategy for stored procedures can be optimized by the server, which will result in the execution of queries occurring more quickly.

4. **Code Reusability:** Stored procedures can be called from various parts of an application or by various applications altogether. This promotes code reusability, reducing the redundancy of code snippets across the codebase.

5. **Transaction Management:** Stored procedures support transaction management, allowing multiple SQL statements to be grouped together as a single transaction. This ensures the atomicity, consistency, isolation, and durability (ACID) properties of transactions.

Creating Stored Procedures

Let's delve into the process of creating stored procedures, examining the syntax and common elements involved. For this illustration, we'll use examples in both MySQL and Microsoft SQL Server.

MySQL Stored Procedure

```
DELIMITER //

CREATE PROCEDURE GetEmployeeDetails (IN employee_id INT)

BEGIN

  SELECT * FROM employees WHERE id = employee_id;

END //

DELIMITER ;
```

In this MySQL example, a stored procedure named **GetEmployeeDetails** is created. It accepts an **employee_id** parameter and retrieves details of the employee with the identified ID from the **employees** table.

Microsoft SQL Server Stored Procedure

```
CREATE PROCEDURE GetEmployeeDetails

    @employee_id INT

AS

BEGIN

    SELECT * FROM employees WHERE id = @employee_id;

END;
```

For Microsoft SQL Server, the syntax is slightly various. The @ symbol denotes a parameter, and the procedure is defined using the **AS BEGIN ... END** block.

Executing Stored Procedures

Once created, stored procedures can be executed using the **CALL** statement in MySQL or the **EXEC** statement in Microsoft SQL Server.

MySQL:

```
CALL GetEmployeeDetails(101);
```

SQL Server:

```
EXEC GetEmployeeDetails @employee_id = 101;
```

Executing these statements will invoke the respective stored procedure and return the details of the employee with the identified ID.

Parameterized Stored Procedures

One of the strengths of stored procedures lies in their ability to accept parameters, enabling dynamic and flexible queries. Parameters allow developers to customize the behavior of stored procedures depending on runtime values.

Instance: Parameterized Stored Procedure

```
CREATE PROCEDURE GetEmployeesByDepartment


  @department_name NVARCHAR(50)
AS
BEGIN
  SELECT * FROM employees WHERE department = @department_name;
END;
```

In this instance, the stored procedure **GetEmployeesByDepartment** accepts a **@department_name** parameter, allowing users to retrieve employees depending on their department.

Advanced Concepts in Stored Procedures

Conditional Logic

Stored procedures support conditional logic, allowing developers to implement branching depending on specific conditions. This can be achieved using **IF...ELSE** statements.

```
CREATE PROCEDURE GetHighSalaryEmployees
  @salary_threshold INT
```

```
AS
BEGIN
  IF @salary_threshold > 50000
  BEGIN
    SELECT * FROM employees WHERE salary > @salary_threshold;
  END
  ELSE
  BEGIN
    SELECT 'Threshold too low';
  END
END;
```

In this instance, the stored procedure checks if the provided **@salary_threshold** is greater than 50,000. If true, it retrieves employees with salaries exceeding the threshold; otherwise, it returns a message.

Loops

While loops and cursor-based loops can be incorporated into stored procedures to iterate over result sets or perform iterative operations.

```
CREATE PROCEDURE ProcessAllEmployees
AS
BEGIN
  DECLARE @employee_id INT;
  DECLARE employee_cursor CURSOR FOR
```

```
    SELECT id FROM employees;

  OPEN employee_cursor;
  FETCH NEXT FROM employee_cursor INTO @employee_id;

  WHILE @@FETCH_STATUS = 0
  BEGIN
     -- Perform operations on employee with ID @employee_id

     FETCH NEXT FROM employee_cursor INTO @employee_id;
  END

  CLOSE employee_cursor;
  DEALLOCATE employee_cursor;
END;
```

This example demonstrates a cursor-based loop that processes each employee in the **employees** table.

Error Handling

Stored procedures can comprise error-handling mechanisms to gracefully handle unexpected situations.

```
CREATE PROCEDURE UpdateEmployeeSalary
  @employee_id INT,
  @new_salary INT
AS
```

```
BEGIN

  BEGIN TRY

    UPDATE employees SET salary = @new_salary WHERE id = @employee_id;

  END TRY

  BEGIN CATCH

    SELECT ERROR_MESSAGE() AS ErrorMessage;

  END CATCH

END;
```

In this instance, the **TRY...CATCH** block captures any errors that may occur during the execution of the update statement.

Executing Stored Procedures from Application Code

Stored procedures are not limited to execution within a database management tool. They can be called from application code written in various programming languages, enabling seamless integration with applications. Let's explore how to execute stored procedures from Python using the **pyodbc** library for SQL Server and the **mysql-connector** library for MySQL.

Executing Stored Procedure from Python (SQL Server)

```
import pyodbc

# Connect to SQL Server
connection = pyodbc.connect('DRIVER={SQL Server};'
            'SERVER=localhost;'
            'DATABASE=YourDatabase;'
            'UID=YourUsername;'
            'PWD=YourPassword')
```

```python
# Create a cursor
cursor = connection.cursor()

# Execute the stored procedure
cursor.execute("{CALL GetEmployeeDetails(?)}", (101,))

# Fetch the result set
result_set = cursor.fetchall()

# Process the result set (print for demonstration purposes)
for row in result_set:
    print(row)

# Close the cursor and connection
cursor.close()
connection.close()
```

Executing Stored Procedure from Python (MySQL)

```python
import mysql.connector
# Connect to MySQL
connection = mysql.connector.connect(
    host='localhost',
    user='YourUsername',
    password='YourPassword',
    database='YourDatabase'
)
# Create a cursor
cursor = connection.cursor()
# Execute the stored procedure
cursor.callproc('GetEmployeeDetails', (101,))
```

```python
# Fetch the result set
result_set = cursor.stored_results()

# Process the result set (print for demonstration purposes)
for result in result_set:
    for row in result.fetchall():
        print(row)

# Close the cursor and connection
cursor.close()
connection.close()
```

In these examples, Python code establishes a connection to the database, creates a cursor, executes the stored procedure, fetches the result set, and processes the data. This illustrates the versatility of stored procedures in being seamlessly integrated into application code.

Best Practices and Considerations

While stored procedures offer numerous advantages, it's essential to follow best practices to ensure their effective utilization and maintainability.

Parameterized Queries

Always use parameterized queries within stored procedures to prevent SQL injection attacks. Avoid concatenating user inputs directly into SQL statements.

```sql
-- Avoid

CREATE PROCEDURE GetEmployeeByName

    @employee_name NVARCHAR(50)

AS
```

```sql
BEGIN

    DECLARE @query NVARCHAR(MAX);

    SET @query = 'SELECT * FROM employees WHERE name = ''' + @employee_name + '''';

    EXEC sp_executesql @query;

END;
-- Prefer
CREATE PROCEDURE GetEmployeeByName

    @employee_name NVARCHAR(50)

AS

BEGIN

    SELECT * FROM employees WHERE name = @employee_name;

END;
```

Transaction Management

Implement transaction management within stored procedures when dealing with multiple SQL statements that should be executed atomically.

```sql
CREATE PROCEDURE TransferFunds

    @from_account INT,

    @to_account INT,

    @amount DECIMAL(10, 2)

AS

BEGIN
```

```sql
BEGIN TRANSACTION;


    UPDATE accounts SET balance = balance - @amount WHERE account_id =
@from_account;

    UPDATE accounts SET balance = balance + @amount WHERE account_id =
@to_account;


    COMMIT;
END;
```

Error Handling

Incorporate robust error-handling mechanisms within stored procedures to gracefully handle unexpected situations and provide meaningful feedback.

```sql
CREATE PROCEDURE InsertEmployee
    @employee_id INT,
    @employee_name NVARCHAR(50)
AS
BEGIN
  BEGIN TRY
     INSERT INTO employees VALUES (@employee_id, @employee_name);
  END TRY
  BEGIN CATCH
```

```
   SELECT ERROR_MESSAGE() AS ErrorMessage;

 END CATCH

END;
```

Documentation

Maintain thorough documentation for stored procedures, comprising details about input parameters, expected outputs, and the purpose of the procedure. This documentation aids other developers and administrators who may interact with the procedures.

Dynamic SQL

Traditional SQL queries are static, meaning the structure and content of the query are known at the time of writing the code. Dynamic SQL, on the other hand, allows for the creation and execution of SQL statements dynamically during runtime. This dynamism brings a new level of flexibility to your queries, enabling you to respond to changing conditions, user inputs, or dynamic data scenarios.

Key Characteristics of Dynamic SQL

1. **Runtime Construction:** Dynamic SQL involves constructing SQL statements during the execution of a program, as opposed to having predefined static queries.

2. **Parameterization:** It often incorporates parameterization to allow for the dynamic inclusion of values, making queries adaptable to varying input conditions.

3. **Versatility:** Dynamic SQL is versatile and can be applied to a wide range of scenarios, comprising dynamic filtering, dynamic column selection, and the creation of complex conditional queries.

4. **Conditional Logic:** It facilitates the incorporation of conditional logic, enabling the generation of various parts of a query depending on runtime conditions.

The Need for Dynamic SQL

- **Adapting to Changing Conditions:** Consider a scenario where you need to build a search functionality for a web application. Users might input various criteria—some might search by name, others by date, and some by a combination of factors. Dynamic SQL allows you to construct a query depending on the user's input, adapting to the changing search conditions dynamically.

- **Dynamic Reporting:** In reporting scenarios, especially when dealing with user-generated reports, the requirements can be dynamic. Users may want to choose specific columns, apply filters conditionally, or sort the data depending on varying criteria. Dynamic SQL empowers you to generate the necessary queries on-the-fly, providing a more responsive and user-centric reporting experience.

- **Database Maintenance and Administration:** Dynamic SQL is also valuable in database maintenance and administration tasks. Consider scenarios where you need to perform actions on multiple tables depending on specific conditions. Dynamic SQL can help you generate the required queries dynamically, streamlining administrative tasks.

Constructing Dynamic SQL

The construction of dynamic SQL involves building SQL statements as strings within the programming language of choice. Let's explore the process using examples in both T-SQL (Microsoft SQL Server) and PL/pgSQL (PostgreSQL).

T-SQL (Microsoft SQL Server)

```
DECLARE @sqlQuery NVARCHAR(MAX);

DECLARE @columnName NVARCHAR(50) = 'employee_name';

DECLARE @searchTerm NVARCHAR(50) = 'John Doe';
```

```
SET @sqlQuery = 'SELECT * FROM employees WHERE ' + @columnName + ' = ''' +
@searchTerm + ''''';

EXEC sp_executesql @sqlQuery;
```

In this T-SQL example, a dynamic SQL query is constructed to select records from the
employees table depending on a dynamic column (**employee_name**) and a dynamic
search term (**John Doe**). The **sp_executesql** procedure is then used to execute the
dynamically constructed query.

PL/pgSQL (PostgreSQL)

```
DO $$

DECLARE

    sqlQuery TEXT;

    columnName TEXT := 'employee_name';

    searchTerm TEXT := 'John Doe';

BEGIN

    sqlQuery := 'SELECT * FROM employees WHERE ' || columnName || ' = ''' || searchTerm
|| '''';


    -- Execute the dynamic query

    EXECUTE sqlQuery;

END $$;
```

In this PL/pgSQL example for PostgreSQL, a dynamic SQL query is constructed similarly. The **EXECUTE** statement is then used to execute the dynamically constructed query.

Parameterization in Dynamic SQL

Parameterization is crucial in dynamic SQL to ensure the secure and efficient inclusion of values. Using parameters helps prevent SQL injection and ensures that values are correctly interpreted. Let's enhance the previous examples with parameterization.

T-SQL with Parameterization

```
DECLARE @sqlQuery NVARCHAR(MAX);

DECLARE @columnName NVARCHAR(50) = 'employee_name';

DECLARE @searchTerm NVARCHAR(50) = 'John Doe';

SET @sqlQuery = 'SELECT * FROM employees WHERE ' + QUOTENAME(@columnName)
+ ' = @searchTerm';

EXEC sp_executesql @sqlQuery, N'@searchTerm NVARCHAR(50)', @searchTerm;
```

In this T-SQL example, the **QUOTENAME** function is used to ensure the correct formatting of the dynamic column name. The **@searchTerm** parameter is then included in the dynamically constructed query.

PL/pgSQL with Parameterization

```
DO $$

DECLARE

  sqlQuery TEXT;

  columnName TEXT := 'employee_name';

  searchTerm TEXT := 'John Doe';
```

```
BEGIN

  sqlQuery := 'SELECT * FROM employees WHERE ' || columnName || ' = $1';


  -- Execute the dynamic query with parameter

  EXECUTE sqlQuery USING searchTerm;

END $$;
```

In this PL/pgSQL example for PostgreSQL, the dynamic column name is concatenated, and the parameter placeholder **$1** is used. The **USING** clause is then employed to pass the parameter value securely.

Dynamic SQL Best Practices

While dynamic SQL offers unparalleled flexibility, it comes with its own set of challenges and considerations. Here are some best practices to ensure effective and secure use of dynamic SQL:

1. **Sanitize User Inputs:** If user inputs are used in constructing dynamic SQL, ensure they are sanitized to prevent SQL injection attacks. Use parameterization or proper escaping methods to handle user inputs safely.

2. **Avoid Concatenation for Sensitive Data:** Avoid directly concatenating sensitive data into dynamic SQL strings. For sensitive data, use parameterization or stored procedures to enhance security.

3. **Parameterize Wherever Possible:** Utilize parameterization for values passed into dynamic SQL. This not only improves security but also ensures correct data typing and interpretation.

4. **Limit Permissions:** Limit the permissions of the user executing dynamic SQL. Avoid granting excessive privileges to prevent potential security risks.

5. **Test Rigorously:** Thoroughly test dynamic SQL queries with various scenarios to ensure they function as intended. Pay special attention to edge cases and unexpected inputs.

6. **Document Dynamically Constructed Queries:** Given the dynamic nature of these queries, maintain detailed documentation outlining the conditions and scenarios under which dynamic SQL queries are constructed.

7. **Monitor Performance:** Keep an eye on the performance of dynamic SQL queries, especially in scenarios where the queries are generated frequently. Assess and optimize as needed.

Dynamic SQL in Application Code

Dynamic SQL is not limited to execution within the database. It can be seamlessly integrated into application code, providing a dynamic and responsive interaction with databases. Let's explore how dynamic SQL can be used in Python with the **pyodbc** library for SQL Server and the **psycopg2** library for PostgreSQL.

Dynamic SQL in Python (SQL Server)

```
import pyodbc

# Connect to SQL Server

connection = pyodbc.connect('DRIVER={SQL Server};'

            'SERVER=localhost;'

            'DATABASE=YourDatabase;'
```

```python
                'UID=YourUsername;'

                'PWD=YourPassword')

# Create a cursor

cursor = connection.cursor()

# Dynamic SQL construction

column_name = 'employee_name'

search_term = 'John Doe'

sql_query = f"SELECT * FROM employees WHERE {column_name} = ?"

# Execute the dynamic query

cursor.execute(sql_query, search_term)

# Fetch the result set

result_set = cursor.fetchall()

# Process the result set (print for demonstration purposes)

for row in result_set:

    print(row)

# Close the cursor and connection

cursor.close()

connection.close()
```

In this Python example using **pyodbc** for SQL Server, a dynamic SQL query is constructed with parameters, and the query is executed with the provided values.

Dynamic SQL in Python (PostgreSQL)

```python
import psycopg2
# Connect to PostgreSQL
connection = psycopg2.connect(
    host='localhost',
    user='YourUsername',
    password='YourPassword',
    database='YourDatabase'
)
# Create a cursor
cursor = connection.cursor()
# Dynamic SQL construction
column_name = 'employee_name'
search_term = 'John Doe'
sql_query = f"SELECT * FROM employees WHERE {column_name} = %s"
# Execute the dynamic query
cursor.execute(sql_query, (search_term,))
# Fetch the result set
result_set = cursor.fetchall()
# Process the result set (print for demonstration purposes)
for row in result_set:
    print(row)
# Close the cursor and connection
cursor.close()
connection.close()
```

In this Python example using **psycopg2** for PostgreSQL, a similar approach is taken to construct and execute a dynamic SQL query.

Transaction Management

A transaction refers to a sequence of one or more SQL statements that are executed as a single unit of work. These statements, when executed together, either succeed as a whole or fail as a whole. The basic purpose of a transaction is to guarantee the database's continuity and integrity while also ensuring that it is accurate, even in the presence of errors or interruptions.

ACID Properties of Transactions

Transactions adhere to a set of principles known as ACID properties, which stand for Atomicity, Consistency, Isolation, and Durability.

1. **Atomicity:** The term "atomic" refers to the fact that a transaction is considered to be a single, unbreakable unit of performance. Each and every one of its functions is carried out, or none of them are. Should any component of the transaction fail, the entire transaction will be reverted to its previous state.

2. **Consistency:** A database can transition from one stable state to an alternate one through the use of transactions. Throughout the process of carrying out a transaction, it is imperative that the integrity restrictions that have been established for the database are not breached.

3. **Isolation:** For the purpose of guaranteeing that the intermediary stage of a transaction is not accessible to other transactions till it is dedicated, every transaction proceeds independently from the other transactions.

4. **Durability:** Following the commitment of a transaction, its impacts become permanent and endure through system failures. The alterations brought about by committed transactions exhibit durability.

Transaction Commands

1. COMMIT

For the purpose of permanently storing the modifications that took place during the current transaction, the COMMIT command is utilized. Following the issuance of a COMMIT, the modifications become irreversible and cannot be undone. COMMIT is the action that guarantees the changes made by a transaction are applied to the database if the transaction is successful.

Example:

```
-- Start a transaction

START TRANSACTION;


-- Perform some operations

UPDATE employees SET salary = salary * 1.1 WHERE department = 'Engineering';


-- Commit the transaction

COMMIT;
```

In this instance, the changes made to the salaries of employees in the Engineering department are committed, making the salary adjustments permanent.

2. ROLLBACK

The ROLLBACK command is used to undo the changes made during the current transaction. It is typically employed when an error occurs, and the changes made by the transaction need to be discarded. ROLLBACK reverts the database to its state prior to the transaction began.

Instance:

```
-- Start a transaction

START TRANSACTION;


-- Perform some operations

UPDATE employees SET salary = salary * 1.1 WHERE department = 'Engineering';


-- Check for an error condition

IF some_error_condition THEN

    -- Roll back the transaction

    ROLLBACK;

ELSE

    -- Commit the transaction

    COMMIT;

END IF;
```

In this instance, a ROLLBACK is triggered if an error condition is detected, ensuring that any changes made within the transaction are discarded.

3. **SAVEPOINT**

SAVEPOINT is a mechanism that allows you to set a point within a transaction to which you can later roll back. It offers a way to create nested transactions or partial rollbacks within a larger transaction.

Instance:

```sql
-- Start a transaction

START TRANSACTION;


-- Perform some operations

UPDATE employees SET salary = salary * 1.1 WHERE department = 'Engineering';


-- Create a savepoint

SAVEPOINT salary_update;


-- Perform additional operations

DELETE FROM employees WHERE department = 'Marketing';


-- Check for an error condition

IF some_error_condition THEN

    -- Roll back to the savepoint

    ROLLBACK TO salary_update;

ELSE

    -- Commit the transaction

    COMMIT;

END IF;
```

In this instance, a SAVEPOINT named **salary_update** is created prior to additional operations. If an error occurs, the transaction is rolled back to this savepoint, undoing only the changes made after the savepoint.

Transaction Control in Practice

1. Simple Transaction

A simple transaction involves a series of operations that either succeed together or fail together. In the case of success, a COMMIT is issued to make the changes permanent. If an error occurs, a ROLLBACK ensures that none of the changes are applied.

Instance:

```
-- Start a transaction
START TRANSACTION;

-- Perform some operations
UPDATE employees SET salary = salary * 1.1 WHERE department = 'Engineering';

-- Check for an error condition
IF some_error_condition THEN
    -- Roll back the transaction
    ROLLBACK;
ELSE
    -- Commit the transaction
    COMMIT;
END IF;
```

In this instance, the salary adjustments are committed if no error occurs, ensuring that the changes are permanent.

2. Nested Transactions with SAVEPOINT

Nested transactions involve creating savepoints within a larger transaction. This allows for partial rollbacks to specific points within the transaction.

Instance:

```
-- Start a transaction
START TRANSACTION;
-- Perform some operations
UPDATE employees SET salary = salary * 1.1 WHERE department = 'Engineering';


-- Create a savepoint
SAVEPOINT salary_update;


-- Perform additional operations
DELETE FROM employees WHERE department = 'Marketing';


-- Check for an error condition
IF some_error_condition THEN
    -- Roll back to the savepoint
    ROLLBACK TO salary_update;
ELSE
    -- Commit the transaction
    COMMIT;
END IF;
```

In this instance, a savepoint named **salary_update** is created prior to additional operations. If an error occurs, the transaction is rolled back to this savepoint, undoing only the changes made after the savepoint.

3. Error Handling with Transactions

Effective error handling is crucial in transactions. It ensures that the database remains in a consistent state even when errors occur.

Instance:

```
-- Start a transaction
START TRANSACTION;


-- Perform some operations
UPDATE employees SET salary = salary * 1.1 WHERE department = 'Engineering';


-- Check for an error condition
IF some_error_condition THEN
    -- Roll back the transaction
    ROLLBACK;
    -- Log the error
    INSERT INTO error_log (error_message) VALUES ('Error updating salaries');
ELSE
    -- Commit the transaction
    COMMIT;
END IF;
```

In this instance, if an error condition is detected, the transaction is rolled back, and an entry is made in the error log. This ensures that the database remains consistent, and errors are appropriately logged for later analysis.

Best Practices for Transaction Management

1. **Keep Transactions Short and Simple:** Avoid long and complex transactions. Short and simple transactions are easier to manage and less prone to errors.

2. **Minimize Lock Duration:** Acquiring locks for an extended period can lead to performance issues. Minimize the duration for which locks are held to improve concurrency.

3. **Use Explicit Transactions:** While some databases support implicit transactions, using explicit transactions (START TRANSACTION, COMMIT, ROLLBACK) enhances code clarity and control.

4. **Implement Error Handling:** Include robust error handling within transactions to gracefully handle unexpected situations and ensure that the database remains in a consistent state.

5. **Test Transactions Rigorously:** Thoroughly test transactions with various scenarios, comprising both successful and error conditions, to ensure they behave as expected.

6. **Choose the Right Isolation Level:** Understand the isolation levels provided by your database system and choose the appropriate level depending on the requirements of your application.

7. **Monitor and Optimize:** Regularly monitor transaction performance and optimize queries within transactions to enhance overall database performance.

Transaction Management in Application Code

Transaction management is not confined to the database alone; it also extends to application code. Let's explore how transactions can be managed in Python using the **pyodbc** library for SQL Server and the **psycopg2** library for PostgreSQL.

Transaction Management in Python (SQL Server)

```python
import pyodbc

# Connect to SQL Server
connection = pyodbc.connect('DRIVER={SQL Server};'
              'SERVER=localhost;'
              'DATABASE=YourDatabase;'
              'UID=YourUsername;'
              'PWD=YourPassword')
# Create a cursor
cursor = connection.cursor()
try:
    # Start a transaction
    connection.autocommit = False
    # Perform some operations
    cursor.execute("UPDATE employees SET salary = salary * 1.1 WHERE department = 'Engineering'")
    # Check for an error condition
    if some_error_condition:
        # Roll back the transaction
        connection.rollback()
    else:
        # Commit the transaction
        connection.commit()
finally:
    # Ensure autocommit is restored
    connection.autocommit = True
# Close the cursor and connection
cursor.close()
connection.close()
```

In this Python example using **pyodbc** for SQL Server, a transaction is initiated by setting **connection.autocommit** to **False**. Operations are performed within the transaction, and a COMMIT or ROLLBACK is executed depending on the success or failure of the transaction.

Transaction Management in Python (PostgreSQL)

```python
import psycopg2

# Connect to PostgreSQL
connection = psycopg2.connect(
    host='localhost',          user='YourUsername',          password='YourPassword',
database='YourDatabase'
)

# Create a cursor
cursor = connection.cursor()
try:
    # Start a transaction
    connection.autocommit = False

    # Perform some operations
    cursor.execute("UPDATE employees SET salary = salary * 1.1 WHERE department = 'Engineering'")

    # Check for an error condition
    if some_error_condition:
        # Roll back the transaction
        connection.rollback()
    else:
        # Commit the transaction
```

```
    connection.commit()
finally:
   # Ensure autocommit is restored
   connection.autocommit = True


# Close the cursor and connection
cursor.close()
connection.close()
```

In this Python example using **psycopg2** for PostgreSQL, a similar approach is taken to manage transactions. The **connection.autocommit** attribute is used to control the transaction state.

4.2 - Integrations: ODBC, JDBC, XML, and JSON in SQL

In this chapter, we explore the integration of SQL with various technologies, expanding the capabilities of your database interactions.

Overview of ODBC and JDBC

What is ODBC?

Open Database Connectivity, commonly known as ODBC, is a standard interface that enables communication between applications and relational database management systems (RDBMS). Developed by Microsoft in the early 1990s, ODBC's primary goal is to provide a universal interface for accessing and interacting with various databases, irrespective of the underlying database management system.

Key Components of ODBC

- **Driver Manager:** The Driver Manager is a crucial component of ODBC that manages communication between applications and ODBC drivers. It facilitates the loading and unloading of ODBC drivers depending on the requirements of the application.

- **ODBC Driver:** The ODBC Driver acts as a mediator between the application and the database. It translates ODBC function calls into commands that the underlying database system can understand. Each database system typically has its own ODBC driver.

- **Data Source:** A Data Source, in the context of ODBC, refers to the connection information and configuration settings needed to establish a link between an application and a specific database. It includes details like the database name, server address, and authentication credentials.

How ODBC Works

1. **Application Requests Connection:** An application initiates a connection by requesting the ODBC Driver Manager to establish a connection to a specific Data Source.

2. **Driver Manager Loads Driver:** The Driver Manager loads the appropriate ODBC driver depending on the identified Data Source. This driver is responsible for handling the communication between the application and the database.

3. **Driver Communicates with Database:** The ODBC driver communicates with the database using the native protocol of the database management system. It translates ODBC function calls into database-specific commands.

4. **Data Exchange:** The application and the database exchange data through the ODBC driver. The driver handles tasks like data retrieval, updating, and transaction management.

5. **Closing the Connection:** Once the application has completed its interaction with the database, it requests the ODBC Driver Manager to close the connection. The Driver Manager unloads the ODBC driver, releasing system resources.

Advantages of ODBC

1. **Platform Independence:** ODBC promotes platform independence, allowing applications to communicate with various databases without modification. As long as an ODBC driver is available for a specific database, applications can seamlessly connect.

2. **Database Agnosticism:** ODBC abstracts the underlying database, making applications agnostic to the type of database being accessed. This flexibility simplifies the development process and allows for easier migration between databases.

3. **Unified API:** ODBC offers a standardized API (Application Programming Interface) that developers can use across various programming languages. This consistency streamlines the development process and enhances code reusability.

Java Database Connectivity (JDBC)

Java Database Connectivity, or JDBC, is a Java-based API that enables Java applications to interact with relational databases.

JDBC serves as a bridge between the Java programming language and various database management systems, providing a standardized way to execute SQL queries, retrieve results, and manage database connections. Developed by Sun Microsystems, JDBC has become an integral part of Java's extensive ecosystem, offering seamless integration with SQL databases.

Components of JDBC

1. **JDBC API:** The JDBC API defines a set of interfaces and classes that Java applications use to interact with databases. It includes classes for starting connections, executing queries, handling transactions, and processing result sets.

2. **JDBC Driver:** JDBC drivers are platform-specific implementations that provide the necessary functionality to connect Java applications with specific database systems. JDBC supports various types of drivers, comprising Type 1 (JDBC-ODBC bridge), Type 2 (Native-API driver), Type 3 (Network Protocol driver), and Type 4 (Thin driver).

3. **JDBC URL:** The JDBC URL is a string that contains the information needed to connect to a specific database. It typically includes details like the database server's address, port number, database name, and authentication credentials.

Working with JDBC

1. **Loading the Driver:** The first step in using JDBC is to load the appropriate JDBC driver using the **Class.forName()** method. This dynamically registers the driver with the **DriverManager**.

```
Class.forName("com.mysql.cj.jdbc.Driver");
```

2. **Establishing a Connection:** JDBC offers the **Connection** interface to establish a connection to the database. The **DriverManager.getConnection()** method is used, passing the JDBC URL and authentication credentials.

```
String url = "jdbc:mysql://localhost:3306/mydatabase";
String username = "user";
String password = "password";
Connection connection = DriverManager.getConnection(url, username, password);
```

3. **Creating Statements:** JDBC supports two types of statements: **Statement** and **PreparedStatement**. These statements are used to execute SQL queries against the database.

```
Statement statement = connection.createStatement();

ResultSet resultSet = statement.executeQuery("SELECT * FROM employees");
```

4. **Processing Result Sets:** Result sets contain the data retrieved from a database query. JDBC offers methods to iterate through result sets and retrieve data.

```
while (resultSet.next()) {
  String name = resultSet.getString("employee_name");
  int salary = resultSet.getInt("salary");
  // Process data
}
```

5. **Handling Transactions:** JDBC facilitates transaction management, allowing the coordination of multiple SQL statements as a cohesive unit of work. The outcome of these transactions depends on the success or failure of the operations, leading to either commitment or rollback.

```
try {

    connection.setAutoCommit(false); // Start transaction

    // Execute SQL statements

    connection.commit(); // Commit transaction

} catch (SQLException e) {

    connection.rollback(); // Rollback in case of an exception

} finally {

    connection.setAutoCommit(true); // Restore auto-commit mode

}
```

6. **Closing Resources:** It is crucial to close JDBC resources, like connections, statements, and result sets, to release database and system resources.

```
resultSet.close();

statement.close();

connection.close();
```

Advantages of JDBC

1. **Platform Independence:** Similar to ODBC, JDBC promotes platform independence. Java applications written with JDBC can seamlessly connect to various databases without modification, provided there is a JDBC driver for the specific database.

186

2. **Integration with Java Ecosystem:** JDBC seamlessly integrates with the broader Java ecosystem, allowing Java developers to leverage its capabilities in conjunction with other Java technologies and frameworks.

3. **Uniform API:** JDBC offers a consistent API that remains the same across various database systems. This uniformity simplifies the development process and makes it easier for developers to switch between databases.

Bridging the Gap

While ODBC and JDBC serve similar purposes—facilitating communication between applications and databases—they cater to various ecosystems. ODBC is predominantly used in the Windows environment, often employed by applications developed using languages like C++ and C#. On the other hand, JDBC is tailored for Java applications and seamlessly integrates with the Java programming language.

ODBC to JDBC Bridging

In scenarios where a non-Java application needs to communicate with a database through JDBC, a bridge can be established. One common approach is using the JDBC-ODBC bridge, which allows ODBC-based applications to utilize JDBC functionality. The JDBC-ODBC bridge is part of the Java Standard Edition and enables ODBC-based applications to connect to any database that has a JDBC driver.

JDBC to ODBC Bridging

Conversely, when a Java application needs to interact with an ODBC-compliant database, bridging from JDBC to ODBC is achievable through third-party tools. These tools act as intermediaries, allowing Java applications to communicate with ODBC databases seamlessly.

SQL and XML Integration

What is XML?

XML, or Extensible Markup Language, is a versatile and human-readable markup language designed to store and transport data. Unlike HTML, which focuses on presentation, XML is specifically crafted for representing structured data. It consists of user-defined tags that describe the content, making it highly flexible and self-descriptive.

Key Features of XML:

1. **Hierarchical Structure:** XML documents are organized in a hierarchical structure, resembling a tree. This inherent hierarchy allows for the representation of complex associations between various pieces of data.

2. **Self-Descriptive Tags:** XML tags are user-defined, making them self-descriptive. This characteristic enhances the readability and understanding of the data being signified.

3. **Platform-Independent:** XML is platform-independent and can be used across various operating systems and programming languages. This portability makes it a preferred choice for data interchange between diverse systems.

4. **Support for Metadata:** XML supports the inclusion of metadata, allowing developers to add information about the structure, encoding, and meaning of the data.

XML Instance:

Consider a simple XML representation of employee data:

```xml
<employees>
  <employee>
    <id>001</id>
    <name>John Doe</name>
    <position>Software Engineer</position>
    <department>Engineering</department>
  </employee>
  <employee>
    <id>002</id>
    <name>Jane Smith</name>
    <position>Data Analyst</position>
    <department>Analytics</department>
  </employee>
</employees>
```

In this instance, the XML document represents a collection of employees, each with attributes like ID, name, position, and department.

Storage

XML Data Type in SQL

Many modern relational database management systems (RDBMS) provide native support for XML data types. SQL standards comprise specific data types, like **XML** or **XMLTYPE**, which allow for the storage of XML documents within the database.

Storing XML in SQL

The process of storing XML in SQL involves creating a column with the appropriate XML data type. Let's consider an example using SQL Server:

```sql
CREATE TABLE EmployeeData (

    EmployeeID INT PRIMARY KEY,

    EmployeeInfo XML

);

INSERT INTO EmployeeData (EmployeeID, EmployeeInfo)

VALUES (

    001,

    '<employee>

        <id>001</id>

        <name>John Doe</name>

        <position>Software Engineer</position>

        <department>Engineering</department>

    </employee>'

);
```

In this instance, a table named **EmployeeData** is created with two columns: **EmployeeID** of type **INT** and **EmployeeInfo** of type **XML**. An XML document is then inserted into the table.

Benefits of Storing XML in SQL:

1. **Consistency and Integrity:** Storing XML data in SQL ensures consistency and integrity, as the database management system enforces data type constraints.

2. **Query and Indexing:** XML data stored in SQL can be queried using SQL's rich set of querying capabilities. Additionally, databases often provide indexing mechanisms to enhance the performance of XML queries.

3. **Transaction Support:** SQL databases offer transaction support for XML data, ensuring that modifications to XML documents are performed atomically.

Querying

XPath in SQL

XPath (XML Path Language) is a query language used for navigating XML documents. SQL standards often incorporate XPath for querying XML data stored in the database.

Instance XPath Query:

Consider querying the **EmployeeData** table to retrieve the names of all employees:

```
SELECT

   EmployeeInfo.value('(//name)[1]', 'nvarchar(100)') AS EmployeeName

FROM

   EmployeeData;
```

In this instance, the **value()** method is used with an XPath expression to extract the name of the first employee from the **EmployeeInfo** XML column.

XQuery in SQL

XQuery, a query language designed specifically for querying XML data, is also supported by some SQL databases.

Instance XQuery Query:

Retrieve the positions of employees using XQuery:

```
SELECT

  EmployeeInfo.query('data(/employee/position)') AS EmployeePosition

FROM

  EmployeeData;
```

In this query, the **query()** method is employed with an XQuery expression to extract the position of each employee.

Benefits of Querying XML in SQL:

1. **Unified Query Language:** SQL offers a unified language for querying both relational and XML data. This consistency simplifies the querying process and allows developers to leverage existing SQL knowledge.

2. **Integration with Relational Data:** SQL's ability to query XML seamlessly alongside traditional relational data promotes integration and enables comprehensive analysis.

3. **Fine-Grained Access Control:** SQL databases often provide fine-grained access control for XML data, allowing administrators to define access permissions depending on specific XML elements or attributes.

Manipulation

Modifying XML Data

SQL allows for the modification of XML data stored in the database. This includes adding, updating, or deleting XML elements or attributes.

Instance Update Statement:

Suppose we want to update the department of an employee:

```
UPDATE EmployeeData

SET EmployeeInfo.modify('replace value of (/employee/department)[1] with "Research"')

WHERE EmployeeID = 001;
```

In this instance, the **modify()** method is used with an XQuery expression to replace the value of the department element for a specific employee.

Benefits of XML Manipulation in SQL:

1. **Consistency Across Data Types:** SQL's support for XML manipulation ensures consistency across various data types within the database, promoting data integrity.

2. **Transaction Support:** XML modifications can be performed within the context of a transaction, ensuring that changes are either committed entirely or rolled back in case of an error.

3. **Auditing and Versioning:** SQL databases often provide auditing and versioning capabilities, allowing for the tracking of changes made to XML data over time.

Challenges and Best Practices

Challenges in SQL and XML Integration:

1. **Performance Considerations:** Processing and querying large XML documents within a relational database can have performance implications. Proper indexing and query optimization are crucial.

2. **Data Validation:** Ensuring the validity and integrity of XML data can be challenging. SQL databases may offer schema validation mechanisms to address this concern.

Best Practices:

1. **Use Native XML Data Types:** Whenever possible, use native XML data types provided by the database management system to benefit from optimized storage and querying.

2. **Optimize Indexing:** Utilize indexing features provided by the database to optimize the performance of XML queries.

3. **Consider Shredding:** In scenarios where XML documents are large and complex, consider shredding them into multiple related tables for better performance and maintainability.

4. **Regular Maintenance:** Regularly perform maintenance tasks, like purging outdated XML data, to keep the database performing efficiently.

JSON in SQL

What is JSON?

JavaScript Object Notation, commonly known as JSON, is a lightweight data interchange format. It is easy for humans to read and write and easy for machines to parse and generate. JSON is language-independent, making it a widely adopted format for representing structured data.

Key Features of JSON

1. **Simple Syntax:** JSON has a straightforward and simple syntax, primarily consisting of key-value pairs, arrays, and nested structures.

2. **Human-Readable:** The format is human-readable and writable, which facilitates ease of understanding and manual editing.

3. **Language Independence:** JSON is independent of programming languages, making it a versatile choice for data interchange between various systems.

4. **Support for Arrays and Objects:** JSON supports both arrays and objects, allowing for the representation of complex data structures.

JSON Instance:

Consider a simple JSON representation of employee data:

```json
{
 "employees": [
  {
   "id": 001,
   "name": "John Doe",
   "position": "Software Engineer",
   "department": "Engineering"
  },
  {
   "id": 002,
   "name": "Jane Smith",
   "position": "Data Analyst",
   "department": "Analytics"
  }
 ]
}
```

In this instance, the JSON document represents a collection of employees, each with attributes like ID, name, position, and department.

Storage

JSON Data Type in SQL

Modern relational database management systems (RDBMS) provide native support for the JSON data type. This allows developers to store JSON documents directly within the database, treating them as first-class citizens.

Storing JSON in SQL:

The process of storing JSON in SQL involves creating a column with the appropriate JSON data type. Let's consider an example using SQL Server:

```
CREATE TABLE EmployeeData (
    EmployeeID INT PRIMARY KEY,
    EmployeeInfo JSON
);


INSERT INTO EmployeeData (EmployeeID, EmployeeInfo)
VALUES (
    001,
    '{"id": 001, "name": "John Doe", "position": "Software Engineer", "department": "Engineering"}'
);
```

In this instance, a table named **EmployeeData** is created with two columns: **EmployeeID** of type **INT** and **EmployeeInfo** of type **JSON**. A JSON document is then inserted into the table.

Benefits of Storing JSON in SQL:

1. **Consistency and Integrity:** Storing JSON data in SQL ensures consistency and integrity, as the database management system enforces data type constraints.

2. **Query and Indexing:** JSON data stored in SQL can be queried using SQL's querying capabilities. Additionally, databases often provide indexing mechanisms to enhance the performance of JSON queries.

3. **Transaction Support:** SQL databases offer transaction support for JSON data, ensuring that modifications to JSON documents are performed atomically.

Querying

JSON Functions in SQL

SQL databases provide a set of functions specifically designed for querying and extracting information from JSON documents.

Instance JSON Query:

Consider querying the **EmployeeData** table to retrieve the names of all employees:

```
SELECT

  JSON_VALUE(EmployeeInfo, '$.name') AS EmployeeName

FROM

  EmployeeData;
```

In this instance, the **JSON_VALUE()** function is used to extract the name of each employee from the **EmployeeInfo** JSON column.

Benefits of Querying JSON in SQL:

- **Unified Query Language:** SQL offers a unified language for querying both relational and JSON data. This consistency simplifies the querying process and allows developers to leverage existing SQL knowledge.

- **Integration with Relational Data:** SQL's ability to query JSON seamlessly alongside traditional relational data promotes integration and enables comprehensive analysis.

- **Fine-Grained Access Control:** SQL databases often provide fine-grained access control for JSON data, allowing administrators to define access permissions depending on specific JSON elements or attributes.

Manipulation

Modifying JSON Data

SQL allows for the modification of JSON data stored in the database. This includes adding, updating, or deleting JSON elements or attributes.

Instance Update Statement:

Suppose we want to update the department of an employee:

```
UPDATE EmployeeData

SET EmployeeInfo = JSON_MODIFY(EmployeeInfo, '$.department', 'Research')

WHERE EmployeeID = 001;
```

In this instance, the **JSON_MODIFY()** function is used to update the value of the department attribute for a specific employee.

Benefits of JSON Manipulation in SQL:

- **Consistency Across Data Types:** SQL's support for JSON manipulation ensures consistency across various data types within the database, promoting data integrity.

- **Transaction Support:** JSON modifications can be performed within the context of a transaction, ensuring that changes are either committed entirely or rolled back in case of an error.

- **Auditing and Versioning:** SQL databases often provide auditing and versioning capabilities, allowing for the tracking of changes made to JSON data over time.

Challenges and Best Practices

Challenges in JSON and SQL Integration:

1. **Performance Considerations:** Processing and querying large JSON documents within a relational database can have performance implications. Proper indexing and query optimization are crucial.

2. **Data Validation:** Ensuring the validity and integrity of JSON data is challenging. SQL databases offer schema validation mechanisms to address this concern.

Best Practices:

- **Use Native JSON Data Types:** If possible, use native JSON data types provided by the database management system to benefit from optimized storage and querying.

- **Optimize Indexing:** Utilize indexing features provided by the database to optimize the performance of JSON queries.

- **Consider Shredding:** In scenarios where JSON documents are large and complex, consider shredding them into multiple related tables for better performance and maintainability.

- **Regular Maintenance:** Regularly perform maintenance tasks, like purging outdated JSON data, to keep the database performing efficiently.

BOOK 5: MASTERING INTEGRATION AND COMPLEX SOLUTIONS

5.1 - Advanced Techniques in Both Python and SQL

In this advanced chapter, we explore techniques that seamlessly integrate Python and SQL, combining their strengths for sophisticated data solutions.

Python and SQL Integration Strategies

Understanding the Synergy

Python: A General-Purpose Language

Python, which is well-known for its readability and versatility, has emerged as a language of choice for a variety of fields, like web development, data science, and machine learning, among others. Its extensive ecosystem of libraries, like Pandas, NumPy, and scikit-learn, makes it a powerful tool for data manipulation, analysis, and visualization.

SQL: The Language of Databases

Structured Query Language (SQL), on the other hand, is specifically designed for managing and manipulating relational databases. SQL enables users to interact with databases, perform queries, insert or update records, and define database structures.

The Need for Integration

While Python excels in data analysis and manipulation, SQL is the language of choice for interacting with databases. Integrating these two worlds becomes crucial when building end-to-end data solutions, where data extraction, transformation, and loading (ETL) processes often involve both Python and SQL components.

Python and SQL Integration Strategies

1. Database API (DB-API)

The Python standard library includes the Database API (DB-API), which serves as a specification for database access modules. Various database connectors, like **sqlite3** for SQLite or **psycopg2** for PostgreSQL, adhere to this standard. Leveraging DB-API, developers can connect to databases, execute SQL queries, and fetch results directly from Python scripts.

Instance Using DB-API (sqlite3):

```python
import sqlite3

# Connect to SQLite database
conn = sqlite3.connect('example.db')

# Create a cursor object
cursor = conn.cursor()

# Execute SQL query
cursor.execute('SELECT * FROM employees')

# Fetch results
results = cursor.fetchall()

# Print results
for row in results:
    print(row)
```

```
# Close the connection
conn.close()
```

In this instance, the **sqlite3** module is used to connect to an SQLite database, execute a simple query, and fetch the results.

2. Object-Relational Mapping (ORM)

ORM frameworks, like SQLAlchemy, provide an abstraction layer that allows developers to interact with databases using Python objects instead of raw SQL. This strategy simplifies database interactions, making the code more readable and maintainable.

Instance Using SQLAlchemy:

```
from sqlalchemy import create_engine, Column, Integer, String, select
from sqlalchemy.ext.declarative import declarative_base
from sqlalchemy.orm import sessionmaker

# Define a SQLAlchemy model
Base = declarative_base()

class Employee(Base):
    __tablename__ = 'employees'
    id = Column(Integer, primary_key=True)
    name = Column(String)
    position = Column(String)
    department = Column(String)

# Create an SQLite in-memory database
engine = create_engine('sqlite:///:memory:')
```

```python
# Create tables
Base.metadata.create_all(engine)

# Create a session
Session = sessionmaker(bind=engine)
session = Session()

# Insert data
session.add_all([
    Employee(name='John Doe', position='Software Engineer', department='Engineering'),
    Employee(name='Jane Smith', position='Data Analyst', department='Analytics')
])
session.commit()

# Query data
query = select(Employee)
results = session.execute(query)

# Print results
for row in results:
    print(row)
```

In this instance, SQLAlchemy is used to define a model, create an SQLite in-memory database, insert data, and query the database using Pythonic syntax.

3. DataFrames and SQL

For data analysis tasks, Pandas DataFrames provide a convenient interface for working with tabular data in Python. The **pandasql** library allows users to run SQL queries directly on Pandas DataFrames, providing a bridge between Python and SQL for data manipulation.

Instance Using pandasql:

```python
import pandas as pd
from pandasql import sqldf

# Create a Pandas DataFrame
data = {
    'id': [1, 2],
    'name': ['John Doe', 'Jane Smith'],
    'position': ['Software Engineer', 'Data Analyst'],
    'department': ['Engineering', 'Analytics']
}
df = pd.DataFrame(data)

# Define a SQL query
query = 'SELECT * FROM df WHERE department = "Engineering"'
# Run the SQL query on the DataFrame
result = sqldf(query, globals())

# Print result
print(result)
```

In this instance, a Pandas DataFrame is created, and a SQL query is executed on the DataFrame using the **pandasql** library.

4. Executing SQL Scripts in Python

Python offers the **subprocess** module, allowing the execution of external processes. This can be utilized to run SQL scripts or command-line SQL tools directly from a Python script.

Instance Using subprocess:

```python
import subprocess

# Define SQL script
sql_script = '''
    SELECT * FROM employees
    WHERE department = 'Engineering';
'''

# Save script to a file
with open('query.sql', 'w') as file:
    file.write(sql_script)

# Execute SQL script using the sqlite3 command-line tool
result = subprocess.run(['sqlite3', 'example.db', '.read query.sql'], capture_output=True, text=True)

# Print result
print(result.stdout)
```

In this instance, a SQL script is defined, saved to a file, and then executed using the **sqlite3** command-line tool via the **subprocess** module.

5. Stored Procedures and Python

Database systems often support the creation of stored procedures, which are sequences of SQL statements stored in the database. Python can interact with these stored procedures by executing them using the appropriate database connector.

Instance Using Stored Procedure and Python:

Assume a stored procedure named **GetEmployees** is defined in the database:

```
CREATE PROCEDURE GetEmployees
AS
BEGIN
    SELECT * FROM employees;
END;
```

Python code to execute the stored procedure:

```python
import pyodbc
# Connect to SQL Server database
conn = pyodbc.connect('Driver={SQL Server};'
            'Server=localhost;'
            'Database=exampledb;'
            'Trusted_Connection=yes;')
# Create a cursor
cursor = conn.cursor()
# Execute the stored procedure
cursor.execute('{CALL GetEmployees}')
# Fetch results
results = cursor.fetchall()
# Print results
for row in results:
```

```
    print(row)
# Close the connection
conn.close()
```

In this instance, Python, using the **pyodbc** library, connects to a SQL Server database and executes a stored procedure named **GetEmployees**.

Best Practices and Considerations

1. **Security:** Always prioritize security when integrating Python and SQL. Use parameterized queries to prevent SQL injection attacks. Ensure that database credentials are securely stored and never hard-coded within scripts.

2. **Performance:** Consider the performance implications of various integration strategies. For large datasets, optimizing SQL queries or utilizing server-side operations may enhance performance.

3. **Compatibility:** Ensure compatibility between Python versions, database connectors, and database systems. Stay informed about updates and changes in libraries to avoid potential compatibility issues.

4. **Maintainability:** Choose an integration strategy that aligns with the maintainability goals of your project. Consider factors like code readability, ease of debugging, and long-term support.

Leveraging Python Libraries with SQL

The Intersection of Python and SQL

- **Python's Rich Ecosystem:** Python's popularity in the data science and machine learning communities stems from its rich ecosystem of libraries. From Pandas for data manipulation to NumPy for numerical computing and scikit-learn for machine learning, Python offers a versatile toolkit for a wide array of data-related tasks.

- **SQL's Database Management Power:** On the other hand, SQL excels in managing and querying relational databases. Its declarative syntax allows for efficient retrieval and manipulation of structured data, making it a staple in database management systems.

- **The Need for Integration:** As data solutions become increasingly complex, the need to seamlessly integrate Python's analytical and machine learning capabilities with SQL's data management strengths becomes paramount. This integration allows for a more holistic approach to data processing, combining the efficiency of SQL in handling structured data with the analytical power of Python.

Leveraging Python Libraries in SQL

1. **Running Python Code in SQL Procedures:** Many relational database management systems now offer extensions that allow the execution of Python code within SQL procedures. This integration enables the creation of stored procedures or functions that leverage Python libraries directly.

Instance Using SQL Server and Python:

Assuming a scenario where a machine learning model is trained using Python and the model needs to be applied within a SQL Server environment:

```sql
-- Define a stored procedure that calls Python code

CREATE PROCEDURE ApplyModel

AS

BEGIN

  EXEC sp_execute_external_script

    @language = N'Python',

    @script = N'
```

```
    # Python code to apply the trained machine learning model

    predictions = model.predict(input_data)

    OutputDataSet = input_data.assign(Predictions=predictions.tolist())
',

    @input_data_1 = N'SELECT * FROM InputData',

    @output_data_1_name = N'OutputDataSet';
END;
```

In this instance, the **sp_execute_external_script** procedure is used in SQL Server to execute Python code, applying a machine learning model to a dataset.

2. **Pandas Integration for Data Manipulation:** Pandas, a powerful data manipulation library in Python, can be integrated with SQL to enhance data processing capabilities. Python scripts leveraging Pandas can be executed within SQL procedures or scripts.

Instance Using Pandas in SQL Server:

```
-- Define a stored procedure that uses Python with Pandas

CREATE PROCEDURE ProcessData

AS

BEGIN

  EXEC sp_execute_external_script

    @language = N'Python',

    @script = N'

      import pandas as pd
```

```
    # Python code using Pandas for data manipulation

    df = pd.read_sql("SELECT * FROM RawData", conn)

    processed_data = df.groupby("category").mean()


    OutputDataSet = processed_data
  '
  ,
  @input_data_1 = N'SELECT * FROM RawData',

  @output_data_1_name = N'OutputDataSet';
END;
```

In this instance, the **sp_execute_external_script** procedure is used to execute Python code with Pandas, reading data from an SQL table, performing data manipulation, and storing the result in another SQL table.

3. **Scikit-Learn for Machine Learning in SQL:** Integrating Scikit-Learn, a machine learning library in Python, with SQL environments allows for the training and application of machine learning models within SQL procedures.

Instance Using Scikit-Learn in SQL Server:

```
-- Define a stored procedure that uses Python with Scikit-Learn
CREATE PROCEDURE TrainAndPredict
AS
BEGIN
  EXEC sp_execute_external_script
    @language = N'Python',
```

```
@script = N'
    from sklearn.model_selection import train_test_split
    from sklearn.ensemble import RandomForestClassifier
    from sklearn.metrics import accuracy_score
    # Python code using Scikit-Learn for machine learning
    X_train, X_test, y_train, y_test = train_test_split(features, labels, test_size=0.2)
    model = RandomForestClassifier()
    model.fit(X_train, y_train)
    predictions = model.predict(X_test)
    accuracy = accuracy_score(y_test, predictions)
    OutputDataSet = data.frame(accuracy=accuracy)
',
@input_data_1 = N'SELECT * FROM TrainingData',
@input_data_2 = N'SELECT * FROM TestData',
@output_data_1_name = N'OutputDataSet';
END;
```

In this instance, the **sp_execute_external_script** procedure is used to execute Python code with Scikit-Learn, training a machine learning model on training data and evaluating its accuracy on test data.

Benefits and Considerations

Benefits of Python and SQL Integration:

- **Comprehensive Data Processing:** Integration allows for comprehensive data processing, leveraging Python's analytical capabilities alongside SQL's data management strengths.

- **Efficient Use of Resources:** Performing data analysis and machine learning directly within the SQL environment avoids the need for data movement between various systems, optimizing resource utilization.

- **Seamless Workflow:** Developers and data professionals can work seamlessly within a unified environment, reducing the complexity of managing multiple tools and systems.

- **Reuse of Existing Code:** Existing Python code, especially in the form of machine learning models or data manipulation scripts, can be reused within SQL procedures, promoting code reusability.

Considerations:

- **Security and Permissions:** Ensure that the execution of Python code within SQL procedures adheres to security best practices. Define appropriate permissions to prevent unauthorized access or execution.

- **Resource Management:** Be mindful of resource usage, especially when running resource-intensive Python code within SQL environments. Consider optimization techniques to balance performance and resource consumption.

- **Compatibility:** Verify the compatibility of Python libraries with the SQL environment. Keep track of library versions and updates to avoid compatibility issues.

- **Testing and Debugging:** Implement robust testing procedures for integrated Python and SQL code. Debugging tools may vary between Python IDEs and SQL environments, requiring a comprehensive testing strategy.

Real-World Applications

1. **Predictive Maintenance in Manufacturing:** Integrating Python libraries with SQL allows for the implementation of predictive maintenance models directly within manufacturing databases. For example, a Scikit-Learn model predicting equipment failures can be trained and applied within the SQL environment, providing real-time insights.

2. **Customer Segmentation in E-Commerce:** Python's Pandas, coupled with SQL, enables the creation of customer segmentation strategies directly within the database. E-commerce platforms can leverage this integration to categorize customers depending on purchasing behavior, facilitating targeted marketing efforts.

3. **Fraud Detection in Finance:** Machine learning models for fraud detection, implemented using Scikit-Learn, can be seamlessly integrated into SQL procedures within financial databases. This integration enhances fraud detection capabilities without the need for data transfers.

Real-world Applications of Integrated Python and SQL Solutions

1: Predictive Analytics in Retail

Background:

A leading retail company sought to enhance its inventory management and optimize supply chain processes. The goal was to predict product demand accurately, minimizing overstock and stockouts. To achieve this, the company aimed to integrate Python's analytical capabilities with its existing SQL-based inventory management system.

Solution:

The solution involved creating a predictive analytics model using Python's Scikit-Learn library to forecast product demand. The model utilized historical sales data stored in the SQL database. An integrated Python and SQL approach was adopted to execute the following steps:

1. **Data Extraction:** Python scripts were employed to extract historical sales data from the SQL database using the Pandas library. This allowed for seamless integration between Python and SQL, minimizing data transfer complexities.

```
import pandas as pd
import pyodbc
```

```
# Connect to SQL Server database
conn = pyodbc.connect('Driver={SQL Server};'
            'Server=localhost;'
            'Database=retail_db;'
            'Trusted_Connection=yes;')
# Query historical sales data
query = 'SELECT * FROM sales_data'
sales_data = pd.read_sql(query, conn)
# Close the connection
conn.close()
```

2. **Data Preprocessing and Feature Engineering:** Python scripts were used to preprocess the data and engineer relevant features for the predictive model. This step involved cleaning data, handling missing values, and creating features like seasonality indicators.

```
# Data preprocessing and feature engineering

# ...
```

3. **Model Training:** The Scikit-Learn library in Python was leveraged to train a machine learning model depending on historical sales patterns. The trained model aimed to predict future demand for each product.

```
from sklearn.model_selection import train_test_split

from sklearn.ensemble import RandomForestRegressor

from sklearn.metrics import mean_squared_error


# Split data into training and testing sets

X_train, X_test, y_train, y_test = train_test_split(features, labels, test_size=0.2)
```

```
# Train a Random Forest Regressor

model = RandomForestRegressor()

model.fit(X_train, y_train)


# Evaluate model performance

predictions = model.predict(X_test)

mse = mean_squared_error(y_test, predictions)
```

4. **Model Integration with SQL:** Once the model was trained and validated, Python scripts were used to integrate the predictive model back into the SQL environment. This integration allowed for real-time predictions within the SQL-based inventory management system.

```
# Save the trained model to a file

joblib.dump(model, 'demand_prediction_model.joblib')


# Connect to SQL Server database

conn = pyodbc.connect('Driver={SQL Server};'

        'Server=localhost;'

        'Database=retail_db;'

        'Trusted_Connection=yes;')
```

```
# Insert the model into the SQL database

with open('demand_prediction_model.joblib', 'rb') as file:

    model_blob = file.read()

query = 'INSERT INTO models (model_name, model_blob) VALUES (?, ?)'

params = ('DemandPredictionModel', model_blob)

conn.execute(query, params)


# Close the connection

conn.close()
```

Outcome:

The integrated Python and SQL solution enabled the retail company to make data-driven decisions in real-time. Predictive analytics, seamlessly integrated into the SQL environment, provided accurate demand forecasts. It was as a consequence of this that inventory levels were optimized, carrying costs were lowered, and general supply chain effectiveness saw an improvement.

2: Fraud Detection in Financial Transactions

Background:

A financial institution faced the challenge of detecting fraudulent transactions within its vast dataset of financial transactions. Traditional SQL queries alone were insufficient to identify complex patterns indicative of fraud. To address this, the institution aimed to integrate Python's machine learning capabilities with its SQL-based transaction database.

Solution:

The solution involved implementing a machine learning model for fraud detection using Python's Scikit-Learn library. The model was trained to identify patterns associated with fraudulent transactions. The integration of Python and SQL was instrumental in achieving the following:

1. **Data Preparation and Feature Engineering:** Python scripts were used to preprocess transaction data extracted from the SQL database. Features like transaction amount, location, and frequency were engineered to enhance the model's ability to detect anomalies.

```
import pandas as pd
import pyodbc
# Connect to SQL Server database
conn = pyodbc.connect('Driver={SQL Server};'
        'Server=localhost;'
        'Database=financial_db;'
        'Trusted_Connection=yes;')
# Query transaction data
query = 'SELECT * FROM transaction_data'
transaction_data = pd.read_sql(query, conn)
# Close the connection
conn.close()
# Data preprocessing and feature engineering
# ...
```

2. **Model Training:** A machine learning model, specifically an Isolation Forest, was trained using the Scikit-Learn library to identify unusual patterns indicative of fraud within the transaction data.

```python
from sklearn.ensemble import IsolationForest

# Train Isolation Forest model

model = IsolationForest(contamination=0.01)

model.fit(transaction_data[['amount', 'frequency', 'location']])
```

3. **Model Integration with SQL:** Python scripts facilitated the integration of the trained model back into the SQL environment. This integration allowed for the real-time application of the fraud detection model to incoming transactions within the SQL database.

```python
# Save the trained model to a file
joblib.dump(model, 'fraud_detection_model.joblib')

# Connect to SQL Server database
conn = pyodbc.connect('Driver={SQL Server};'
            'Server=localhost;'
            'Database=financial_db;'
            'Trusted_Connection=yes;')

# Insert the model into the SQL database
with open('fraud_detection_model.joblib', 'rb') as file:
  model_blob = file.read()
query = 'INSERT INTO models (model_name, model_blob) VALUES (?, ?)'
params = ('FraudDetectionModel', model_blob)
conn.execute(query, params)
# Close the connection
conn.close()
```

Outcome:

The integrated Python and SQL solution provided the financial institution with an advanced fraud detection mechanism. By leveraging Python's machine learning capabilities within the SQL environment, the institution could efficiently analyze and identify fraudulent transactions in real-time. This proactive approach resulted in a significant reduction in financial losses attributed to fraud.

3: Customer Segmentation in E-Commerce

Background:

An e-commerce platform aimed to enhance its marketing strategies by tailoring promotions and recommendations to specific customer segments. The goal was to identify distinct customer segments depending on purchasing behavior. To achieve this, the e-commerce platform sought to integrate Python's Pandas library with its SQL-based customer database.

Solution:

The solution involved leveraging Python's Pandas library for data manipulation and analysis within the SQL environment. The integrated approach facilitated the following steps:

1. **Data Extraction and Preprocessing:** Python scripts were used to extract customer data from the SQL database and preprocess it for segmentation analysis. This involved aggregating purchase history, calculating key metrics, and handling any missing or inconsistent data.

```
import pandas as pd
import pyodbc
# Connect to SQL Server database
conn = pyodbc.connect('Driver={SQL Server};'
            'Server=localhost;'
            'Database=ecommerce_db;'
            'Trusted_Connection=yes;')
```

```
# Query customer data
query = 'SELECT * FROM customer_data'
customer_data = pd.read_sql(query, conn)
# Close the connection
conn.close()
# Data preprocessing for segmentation
# ...
```

2. **Customer Segmentation with Pandas:** Python scripts, utilizing Pandas functionalities, were employed to perform customer segmentation analysis. This involved clustering customers depending on their purchasing behavior, creating distinct segments for targeted marketing strategies.

```
# Customer segmentation using Pandas
# ...
```

3. **Segmentation Results Integration with SQL:** The results of the segmentation analysis, comprising assigned segment labels for each customer, were integrated back into the SQL customer database. This integration facilitated the seamless utilization of segmentation information within the e-commerce platform's SQL-based marketing workflows.

```
# Connect to SQL Server database
conn = pyodbc.connect('Driver={SQL Server};'
          'Server=localhost;'
          'Database=ecommerce_db;'
          'Trusted_Connection=yes;')

# Insert segmentation results into the SQL database
```

```
segmentation_results.to_sql('customer_segments',    con=conn,    if_exists='replace',
index=False)


# Close the connection

conn.close()
```

Outcome:

The integrated Python and SQL solution empowered the e-commerce platform to tailor its marketing efforts effectively. Customer segmentation, performed seamlessly within the SQL environment using Python's Pandas library, allowed the platform to target specific customer segments with personalized promotions. This approach resulted in improved customer engagement and increased conversion rates.

5.2 - Conclusion: The Power of Python and SQL: A Journey's End

As we conclude this comprehensive exploration of Python and SQL, it's essential to reflect on the remarkable learning journey we've undertaken. The milestones achieved and the depth of understanding gained have laid a solid foundation for navigating the intricate landscapes of these powerful technologies.

Reflecting on the Learning Journey: Milestones and Achievements

Our journey began with the fundamental concepts of Python, unraveling its syntax, features, and the philosophy that defines its design. We delved into the intricacies of setting up the development environment, ensuring that every aspiring programmer is equipped with the necessary tools to embark on their Python adventure. The hands-on approach to writing the first Python program marked a significant milestone, bridging the gap between theory and practical application.

Navigating Python's syntax became an exhilarating experience as we explored indentation rules, variable declarations, and the fundamental building blocks of the language. The journey continued with a deep dive into algorithms, logical thinking, and the principles of object-oriented programming, unraveling the complexities that underpin effective problem-solving in the programming realm.

Understanding hardware and software foundations became imperative prior to venturing further into the world of Python programming. A primer on computer components and an exploration of essential tools and platforms set the stage for a holistic understanding of the interconnected elements that contribute to seamless coding experiences.

Configuring programming environments, exploring Hello World programs, and grasping the intricacies of variables and data types added layers to our programming expertise. We navigated through Python's versatile data structures, comprising lists, tuples, and dictionaries, understanding their nuances and applicability in various scenarios.

The journey through control flow constructs, like if-else statements and loops, equipped us with the skills to efficiently control program execution and automate repetitive tasks. We ventured into the realm of functions, appreciating their role as the backbone of modular and reusable code. The exploration extended to object-oriented principles, where we embraced encapsulation, inheritance, and polymorphism, laying the groundwork for scalable and intuitive code design.

The Future Awaits: Continuing the Python and SQL Adventure

As we stand at the conclusion of this journey, it's essential to recognize that our exploration of Python and SQL is not merely a conclusion but a transition to the next phase of growth and innovation. The skills acquired form a solid basis for tackling real-world challenges and contributing meaningfully to the ever-evolving landscape of technology.

Looking ahead, the integration of Python and SQL emerges as a pivotal theme. The case studies we explored showcased how the fusion of Python's analytical prowess with SQL's robust data management capabilities can yield transformative solutions. Predictive analytics, fraud detection, and customer segmentation exemplify the real-world applications where this integration shines.

The synergy between Python and SQL opens doors to a multitude of possibilities. Whether it's leveraging Python libraries within SQL environments for advanced analytics or seamlessly integrating Python and SQL for comprehensive data solutions, the future promises a landscape where the boundaries between these technologies blur, giving rise to a more interconnected and powerful ecosystem.

Continuing the Python and SQL adventure involves staying abreast of evolving technologies and industry trends. The integration of Python and SQL is not a static achievement but a dynamic journey that evolves with the technological landscape. As new libraries, frameworks, and methodologies emerge, the adept Python and SQL practitioner remains agile, ready to adapt and innovate.

The integration of Python and SQL stands as a testament to the symbiotic association between programming and data management. The journey we've undertaken is not an end but a stepping stone towards mastery and continuous learning. As you embark on your own Python and SQL adventure, remember that the road ahead is filled with opportunities to create, innovate, and contribute to the transformative power of technology. The future awaits, and with Python and SQL as your companions, the possibilities are boundless.

Appendices

Python Exercises & Projects

Hands-On Python Challenges: Applying Knowledge

1. String Manipulation

Objective: Practice string manipulation skills by creating a program that reverses a given string.

Instructions:

1. Write a Python function that takes a string as input.

2. Reverse the characters of the string.

3. Return the reversed string.

Instance:

```python
def reverse_string(input_str):

    # Your code here


result = reverse_string("Python")

print(result)  # Output: "nohtyP"
```

2. List Comprehension

Objective: Enhance your understanding of list comprehensions by filtering and transforming data.

Instructions:

1. Create a list of numbers from 1 to 10.

2. Use list comprehension to create a new list containing the squares of even numbers.

Instance:

```
original_list = [1, 2, 3, 4, 5, 6, 7, 8, 9, 10]

squares_of_evens = [x**2 for x in original_list if x % 2 == 0]


print(squares_of_evens)  # Output: [4, 16, 36, 64, 100]
```

3. File Handling

Objective: Practice reading and writing to files.

Instructions:

1. Create a text file with some sample text.

2. Write a Python program to read the content of the file and count the occurrences of each word.

3. Display the word count.

Instance:

```
# Assume a file named 'sample.txt' with content: "This is a sample text. This text is for the
Python challenge."


# Your code here


# Output: {'This': 2, 'is': 2, 'a': 1, 'sample': 1, 'text.': 1, 'text': 1, 'for': 1, 'the': 1, 'Python': 1,
'challenge.': 1}
```

Python Project Showcase: Building Practical Applications

1. To-Do List Application

Objective: Build a simple To-Do List application to manage tasks.

Features:

- Add tasks with due dates.
- Mark tasks as completed.
- View a list of pending tasks.
- View completed tasks.

Implementation:

```
# Your implementation here

# Utilize classes, lists, and functions to manage tasks and their statuses.
```

2.Weather Forecast App using API

Objective: Create a weather forecast application that fetches data from a weather API.

Features:

- Input city name from the user.
- Fetch weather data using an API (e.g., OpenWeatherMap API).
- Display current temperature, weather conditions, and forecast.

Implementation:

```
# Your implementation here

# Utilize requests library to make API calls and present weather information to the user.
```

3. Web Scraper for News Headlines

Objective: Build a web scraper that extracts news headlines from a news website.

Features:

- Scrape headlines from a news website (e.g., BBC News).
- Display the headlines to the user.

Implementation:

```
# Your implementation here

# Utilize BeautifulSoup or Scrapy for web scraping and present the headlines to the user.
```

4. Basic Flask Web Application

Objective: Develop a simple web application using Flask.

Features:

- Create a web page with a form.
- Accept user input through the form.
- Process the input and display results on a new page.

Implementation:

```
# Your implementation here

# Utilize Flask for creating web routes, handling forms, and rendering pages.
```

5. Data Visualization with Matplotlib

Objective: Explore data visualization by creating plots and charts.

Features:

- Load a dataset (e.g., CSV file).
- Create various plots, like bar charts, line charts, and scatter plots.

Implementation:

```
# Your implementation here

# Utilize Matplotlib library for data visualization.
```

SQL Exercises & Projects

SQL Skill Challenges: Testing Proficiency

1. Basic Querying

Objective: Test your proficiency in writing basic SQL queries.

Instructions:

1. Write an SQL query to retrieve all columns from a table named **employees**.

2. Write a query to fetch distinct values from a column named **department** in the same table.

Instance:

```
-- Your queries here


-- Instance Output 1: All columns from 'employees'

SELECT * FROM employees;


-- Instance Output 2: Distinct values from 'department'

SELECT DISTINCT department FROM employees;
```

2. Aggregation and Grouping

Objective: Practice using aggregate functions and grouping.

Instructions:

1. Write a query to calculate the average salary for each department.

2. Find the total number of employees in each department.

Instance:

```
-- Your queries here


-- Instance Output 1: Average salary for each department

SELECT department, AVG(salary) AS avg_salary

FROM employees

GROUP BY department;


-- Instance Output 2: Total number of employees in each department

SELECT department, COUNT(*) AS total_employees

FROM employees

GROUP BY department;
```

3. Joins

Objective: Test your skills in performing joins between tables.

Instructions:

1. Write a query to retrieve the names of employees and their corresponding department names from two tables: **employees** and **departments**.

2. Find the total sales amount for each customer from tables **customers** and **orders**.

Instance:

```
-- Your queries here


-- Instance Output 1: Names of employees and their department names

SELECT employees.employee_name, departments.department_name

FROM employees

JOIN departments ON employees.department_id = departments.department_id;


-- Instance Output 2: Total sales amount for each customer

SELECT customers.customer_name, SUM(orders.order_amount) AS total_sales

FROM customers

JOIN orders ON customers.customer_id = orders.customer_id

GROUP BY customers.customer_name;
```

1. Employee Management System

Objective: Design a database system to manage employee information.

Features:

- Create tables for employees, departments, and roles.
- Implement associations between tables.
- Write queries to retrieve employee details, department-wise employee count, etc.

Instance:

-- Your implementation here

-- Tables: employees, departments, roles

-- Instance Query 1: Retrieve employee details

SELECT employee_id, employee_name, department_name, role_name, salary

FROM employees

JOIN departments ON employees.department_id = departments.department_id

JOIN roles ON employees.role_id = roles.role_id;

-- Instance Query 2: Department-wise employee count

SELECT department_name, COUNT(*) AS total_employees

FROM employees

```
JOIN departments ON employees.department_id = departments.department_id

GROUP BY department_name;
```

2. Online Retail Database

Objective: Create a database for an online retail store.

Features:

- Tables for customers, products, orders, and payments.
- Define associations and constraints.
- Implement queries to retrieve customer purchase history and product popularity.

Instance:

```
-- Your implementation here
-- Tables: customers, products, orders, payments

-- Instance Query 1: Customer purchase history
SELECT    customers.customer_name,    products.product_name,    orders.order_date,
payments.payment_amount
FROM customers
JOIN orders ON customers.customer_id = orders.customer_id
JOIN payments ON orders.order_id = payments.order_id
JOIN order_details ON orders.order_id = order_details.order_id
JOIN products ON order_details.product_id = products.product_id;
-- Instance Query 2: Product popularity
SELECT product_name, COUNT(*) AS total_purchases
FROM order_details
JOIN products ON order_details.product_id = products.product_id
```

```
GROUP BY product_name
ORDER BY total_purchases DESC;
```

3. Library Management System

Objective: Develop a database system for managing a library.

Features:

- Tables for books, authors, borrowers, and transactions.
- Establish associations and constraints.
- Write queries to track overdue books, popular authors, etc.

Instance:

```
-- Your implementation here
-- Tables: books, authors, borrowers, transactions
-- Instance Query 1: Overdue books
SELECT books.book_title, borrowers.borrower_name, transactions.due_date
FROM transactions
JOIN books ON transactions.book_id = books.book_id

JOIN borrowers ON transactions.borrower_id = borrowers.borrower_id

WHERE    transactions.return_date    IS    NULL    AND    transactions.due_date    <
CURRENT_DATE;


-- Instance Query 2: Popular authors

SELECT authors.author_name, COUNT(*) AS total_books_published

FROM authors
```

```
JOIN books ON authors.author_id = books.author_id

GROUP BY authors.author_name

ORDER BY total_books_published DESC;
```

Did You Enjoy the Journey?

As you turn this final page, we hope our book has both informed and inspired you.

If it has, please consider sharing your experience with a quick review.

Your honest feedback is not only deeply valued but also guides others in their reading choices.

Thank you for your time and thoughts!

Warmly,

Alan P. Cochran

Recommended Resources and Further Reading

Books

1. **"Python Crash Course" by Eric Matthes:** An impressive resource for beginners, covering Python fundamentals and hands-on projects.

2. **"Fluent Python" by Luciano Ramalho:** Ideal for intermediate Python developers, exploring the language's advanced features and best practices.

3. **"SQL Performance Explained" by Markus Winand:** A comprehensive guide to optimizing SQL performance, suitable for both beginners and experienced developers.

4. **"Learning SQL" by Alan Beaulieu:** A beginner-friendly book that covers SQL basics, database design, and practical examples.

5. **"Clean Code: A Handbook of Agile Software Craftsmanship" by Robert C. Martin:** Essential reading for any programmer, emphasizing clean, maintainable code practices.

Websites

1. Python.org: The official Python website offers documentation, tutorials, and updates on the language.

2. Real Python: A platform with a plethora of tutorials, articles, and resources for Python developers at all skill levels.

3. W3Schools SQL Tutorial: An interactive online resource providing comprehensive SQL tutorials and exercises.

4. SQLZoo: A great interactive platform for practicing SQL through a variety of exercises and challenges.

Courses

1. Coursera - "Python for Everybody" by the University of Michigan: A specialization covering Python basics to web development and databases.

2. edX - "Introduction to Computer Science and Programming Using Python" by MIT: A comprehensive course from MIT, covering Python programming and computer science concepts.

3. Coursera - "SQL for Data Science" by the University of California, Irvine: A specialization focusing on SQL for data analysis and manipulation.

4. Udacity - "Full Stack Web Developer Nanodegree": A hands-on program covering Python, SQL, and web development skills.

5. LinkedIn Learning - Python and SQL Courses: Offers a variety of courses for Python and SQL, ranging from beginner to advanced levels.

Online Platforms

1. GitHub: Explore open-source Python projects and SQL scripts to learn from real-world examples.

2. Stack Overflow: A vibrant community where you can seek help, share knowledge, and learn from experienced developers.

3. LeetCode - SQL Problems: Sharpen your SQL skills by solving problems on LeetCode.

4. Kaggle: Engage in Python and SQL projects related to data science and machine learning.

Continuous learning is crucial in the ever-evolving landscape of programming. These resources provide a diverse range of learning materials, from books and websites to courses and online platforms. Whether you're a beginner or an experienced developer, embracing a variety of learning methods will enhance your skills and keep you at the forefront of technology. Happy learning!

>> BONUS <<

To complete your journey through the fascinating world of Python and SQL, we're excited to offer you some special resources to enhance your learning experience. We've designed a unique workbook featuring 25 carefully crafted multiple-choice quizzes for each chapter to test your understanding and reinforce the key concepts you've learned.

Additionally, to further aid your mastery of Python and SQL, we've selected a range of flashcard decks from the web and some extra exercises and projects. The flashcards will provide you with a dynamic way to review and drill down on technical concepts and questions, making your learning process both efficient and engaging.

To access these valuable tools, simply scan the QR code located below. We've prepared these bonuses specifically for you, to ensure that your learning journey is not only educational but also interactive and fun. Keep practicing and enjoy the journey!

Download Here

Glossary of Terms

>>>

This is the prompt that is displayed by default in the Python interactive shell. All of our examples have shown us a great deal of this.

...

When inputting code inside a pair of matching delimiters or under an intended block, the default prompts of the Python interactive shell are displayed. The use of parentheses, curly braces, or square brackets are all examples of delimiters. Additionally, this is referred to as the ellipsis object.

2to3

Python 3.x is where the future lies, despite the fact that the majority of programs that are currently in existence have their foundation in Python 2.x. The code from version 2.x is not entirely compatible with version 3.x.The fact that we have a tool at our disposal that will assist us in converting Python 2.x code to Python 3.x is rather interesting. The incompatibilities are handled by 2to3, which has the capability to detect them by parsing the source and traversing the parse tree. These are referred to as lib2to3 in the standard library.

Abstract Base Class

It is possible to define interfaces through the use of an abstract base class. It is a good complement to duck typing in this way. When it comes to this, we have the ABC module. It provides virtual subclasses, which are classes that are identified by the is instance () and is subclass () methods, but aren't derived from any other class. Make use of the collections.abc module for data structures, the numbers module for numbers, and the IO module for streams. Python comes with a set of built-in ABCs for data structures, numbers, and streams. Importing finders and loaders is another option (the importlib.abc module is required for this). We also make use of the ABC module in order to design our very own ABCs.

Algorithm

A series of instructions that are supposed to be followed in order to accomplish a certain task or to find a solution to a certain issue. Algorithms are fundamental to computer science and programming.

API (Application Programming Interface)

A set of rules and tools that facilitates communication between various software applications. APIs define the methods and data formats applications can use to request and exchange information.

ASCII (American Standard Code for Information Interchange)

Is a character encoding standard used to signify text in computers, communication equipment, and other devices. In ASCII, each character is assigned a unique numeric value..

Backend

Refers to the server-side of a web application, where data processing, storage, and management occur. The backend is responsible for handling requests from the frontend and interacting with databases.

Boolean

A data type that has only two possible values: true or false. Booleans are commonly used in programming for making logical decisions.

Bug

An error, flaw, or unintended behavior in a software program. Bugs can lead to unexpected results and are typically resolved through debugging.

Class

A blueprint for creating objects in object-oriented programming. A class defines a set of attributes and behaviors that its instances, or objects, will have.

Code

A set of instructions written in a programming language to perform a specific task or function. Code is executed by a computer to produce the desired output.

Coercion

The interpreter implicitly changes one data type to another whenever we do out operations such as adding those two numbers together. It first converts 2 to 2.0 (int to float), and then it adds 3.7 to the result of that conversion. This is referred to as coercion, and if we did not have it, we would have to do it in the following manner intentionally:

```
>>> float(2)+3.7

5.7
```

Compiler

A program responsible for converting source code written in a high-level programming language into either machine code or an intermediate code, enabling execution on a computer.

CRUD (Create, Read, Update, Delete)

A set of basic operations performed on data in a database. CRUD represents the four fundamental functions in database management systems.

CSS (Cascading Style Sheets)

A style sheet language used for describing the presentation of a document written in HTML or XML. CSS defines how elements should be displayed on a web page.

Database

A structured collection of data that is organized and stored electronically. Databases can be relational, NoSQL, or other types, and they play a crucial role in data management.

Debugging

The process of identifying and resolving errors, bugs, or issues in software code is known as debugging. Debugging is essential for ensuring the correct functionality of a program.

Declaration

In programming, the act of introducing an identifier (like a variable or function) to the compiler, specifying its data type and other relevant details.

Dependency

In software development, a association between two modules, where changes in one module may affect the behavior of another module.

Exception

An event that takes place during the execution of a program, causing a deviation from the normal flow of instructions. Exceptions are often handled using try-catch blocks to prevent program crashes.

Frontend

Refers to the client-side of a web application, where the user interacts with the interface. The frontend is responsible for presenting data and sending user requests to the backend.

Function

A section of code that can be reused and is meant to carry out a particular task or collections of tasks. Functions are essential for code organization and reusability.

Git

During the process of software development, a distributed version control system is utilized to monitor and record changes made to the source code. Git enables collaborative coding and offers tools for managing code repositories.

GUI (Graphical User Interface)

A sort of user interface that enables users to interact with electronic devices through the use of graphical components like windows, buttons, and icons. GUIs are common in modern software applications.

HTML (Hypertext Markup Language)

The standard markup language for creating and designing web pages. HTML serves as the foundational language for structuring content on the web, playing a crucial role in the construction of websites.

IDE (Integrated Development Environment)

A software application that furnishes programmers with extensive tools and capabilities for software development. IDEs typically comprise code editors, debuggers, and build automation tools.

Inheritance

In object-oriented programming, the mechanism of creating a new class (derived or child class) from an existing class (base or parent class). The derived class inherits attributes and behaviors from the base class.

Interface

A set of rules or protocols that define how software components should interact. Interfaces ensure consistency and standardization in programming.

JavaScript

A high-level, interpreted programming language predominantly employed for generating dynamic content on the web. JavaScript is commonly employed in frontend development.

Loop

A control flow construct enabling the repeated execution of a set of instructions until a identified condition is satisfied. Loops play a crucial role in automating repetitive tasks within programming.

Method

A class-associated function is a type of function that is used in object-oriented programming. The behavior of objects that are produced from a class is defined by an object's methods.

Object

A container that is self-contained and contains both data and methods to manipulate the data that it holds. Within the realm of object-oriented programming, objects are known as instances of classes.

Operator

A symbol in a programming language that carries out an operation on one or more operands. Common operators comprise +, -, *, /, and =.

Python

A programming language characterized by its high-level nature, interpreted execution, and renowned for its readability and simplicity. Python finds extensive application in web development, data analysis, artificial intelligence, and various other domains.

Repository

A central location where data is stored and managed. In version control systems like Git, a repository holds the history and various versions of a software project.

SQL (Structured Query Language)

A domain-specific language utilized for the management and manipulation of relational databases. SQL offers commands for creating, retrieving, updating, and deleting data.

Syntax

The programming structure of a specific coding element. It is the grammar of programming.

Token

The smallest individual unit in a program written in a programming language. Tokens can be keywords, identifiers, literals, or operators.

Tuple

A sequentially arranged assortment of elements, akin to a list, but unalterable in Python. Tuples are commonly used for grouping related data.

URL (Uniform Resource Locator)

A reference or address used to access resources on the internet. URLs specify the location of web pages, documents, images, and other online content.

Variable

A symbolic name or identifier associated with a value in a program. Variables are used to store and manipulate data during the execution of a program.

Web Development

The act of creating and sustaining websites or web applications. Web development involves frontend development, backend development, and database management.

XML (Extensible Markup Language)

A markup language starting guidelines for encoding documents in a format intelligible to both humans and machines. XML is frequently employed for facilitating data interchange.

Printed in Great Britain
by Amazon

40782610R00139